RAVEN SMITH'S MEN

RAVEN SMITH

4th ESTATE • London

For Richard, I guess

4th Estate
An imprint of HarperCollins*Publishers*
1 London Bridge Street
London SE1 9GF

www.4thEstate.co.uk

HarperCollins*Publishers*
Macken House, 39/40 Mayor Street Upper
Dublin 1, D01 C9W8, Ireland

First published in Great Britain in 2022 by 4th Estate
This 4th Estate paperback edition published in 2023

1

A catalogue record for this book is
available from the British Library

ISBN 9780008457532

Set in Adobe Garamond Pro
Printed and bound in the UK using 100%
renewable electricity at CPI Group (UK) Ltd

MIX
Paper | Supporting
responsible forestry
FSC™ C007454

This book is produced from independently certified FSC™ paper
to ensure responsible forest management.

For more information visit: www.harpercollins.co.uk/green

Contents

Foreword

Herein lie the men of Raven Smith. My men, of course, not yours. Each of them has left a mark, a memory, a stain, whether they meant to or not. Some hit deep, and I caught feels. Some I discarded like a clip-on neck tie. Some I know by blood, others by employment. These chaps have either wound me up or let me down, either wheedling their way under my skin or being rather pleasantly granted access. Maybe the guy was funny, or tall, or implausibly charming? Maybe the guy was none of those but he tossed me off? Maybe he left me breathless? Or left me cold? Some of them clapped my cheeks, while others clapped themselves on their backs. There have been disc jockeys and knob jockeys. Sad sacks and nutsacks. There have been amateur sociologists, privilege apologists and the occasional scatologist. There are stepdads and actual dads, and some who just want to be called 'daddy'. Speaking of which, some were sports dads, ripped and gladiatorial, where others felt vaguely diseased, verging on cadaverous. I still don't know the exact criteria for inclusion in this book, what made me commit some men, but not others, to paper.

There's no empirical formula, no easy equation. I know I never wanted to lump types of men together like curds in a split sauce. I wanted to taste each one separately.

And every time I sat down to write this introduction I could feel myself making excuses for my fixation on men, a need to explain how I became so enthralled, to illustrate why I'm still so engrossed.

Maybe they got to me young, these men, before the charcoal masks, and sleep gummies and expensive artisanal shirts? Maybe I didn't wear enough blue as a baby, or maybe I wore too much? My mum breastfed me until I was four years old (this is the first and last time I will ever speak on this)* so maybe there's something in that? I want to both absolve myself from the guilt of thoroughly enjoying men and their mess, and I also genuinely want to enjoy them guilt-free, without apologising (not saying sorry is known as the Tory MP approach). I'm aware that once you start talking about men and masculinity things can very quickly descend into a *serious discussion*, a *proper talk*, but I must say I've also had a lot of fun with men, and even more fun being one.

I didn't intend to centre men in my memoir, it was meant to be a chapter about my childhood, followed by a chapter

---

* Okay I'm still speaking on this because my mum read the final draft and said I only did eighteen months on the teat tops. Which is probably fine, development-wise? Maybe she's lying to herself? Maybe it's a self-denial we both need? Also, my MySpace bio still says 'My mum breastfed me till I was four' and I don't have the login to change it.

about me, followed by another chapter about how special I am. Perhaps a micro-chapter about my husband or my cat or the Internet for balance. But men are hiding in every memory, every personal recollection. They dominate elsewhere too – in culture and finance, in economics and politics – they are the his in history. My hackles go up along with yours, but, from where I stand, I can see that masculinity is both freeing and limiting, that traditional male qualities – strength, courage, leadership, independence – are also constructed and fallible. Being a man is never net good or net bad.

This book isn't so much for men, as about them. I've been trying to nutshell what it is about them that has kept me intrigued my whole life. It boils down to three things. Firstly, I love them. Secondly, I can see how bottomlessly problematic they are. Thirdly, both these things converge in my own sense of self, my own masculinity.

I can only talk from first-hand experience, where the personal, the primal and the perennial intertwine. I want to look at my own history without flinching, to excavate things I've buried, and trap my lifetime of manliness in amber for inspection. Expect softbois, hard truths and a rigorous retelling of every time I've been punched or fingered.

You have your own men, of course, in all their infuriating, labyrinthine complexity. In the following essays, you get to meet mine.

Fuck Men

I love men so much but, fuck me, they're annoying. I'm really careful to try and balance the pros and cons of masculinity, to be considered and unbiased, even-handed and level-headed, but sometimes men just get on my tits. I'm none of the insults that have been lobbied at feminists over the years. I'm not anti-men, I'm not a sexless, finger-wagging shrew, I'm not a bitch or a prude. At the same time, I completely understand the appeal of those positions, of a man-less celibacy. Shrews do not need taming: ditching men is rather shrewd.

As I traipse this planet, sometimes strutting like Carrie in her knickers before she falls on the runway, sometimes keeping my head down and my headphones in, administering euphoric pop songs as antidepressants, men still find a way to get on my nerves. Men are more annoying than fully-English people saying 'pourquoi?' in a fully-English conversation, or those grown adults who talk in a baby voice, or people with 'dreamer' in their bio. I've had just about all I can manage of men and their bullshit. I collect male transgressions like tourist souvenirs, a snowglobe for each irritation, a fridge magnet for every time they've wound me up. I could do you a Jack the Ripper tour of male misdemeanours. Sometimes a man will sit next to me on the tube with his knees so far apart it's like he has the Taj Mahal in his pants and his nuts are bowling balls. Sometimes groups of men Stonehenge public pavements, nursing beers and refusing to gently ease themselves out of my path. There was a guy recently at the swimming pool who, on seeing I was drying myself with a pink towel, called me brave. During the scramble to deboard a plane, there was an un-tall guy stage-whispering under his breath about my bag's hierarchy in the overhead system. It does always seem to be a man that's exerting a commentary on how my own masculinity sits in a space. Sometimes it's verbal, sometimes not. A man will flex his manliness – invisibly or visibly, consciously or not – penetrating a situation with some male vigour. It is, frankly, exhausting.

I like the club sandwich of human life – the men, the women, the inbetweeners, the undecided – gender is both a contradictory and complementary blend of flavours. But the male ingredient is dominant, like stilton in a crème caramel, and I can never get the taste out of my mouth, there is no adequate palate cleanser. There's no escaping men's thick Philadelphia spread coating all of our tongues. A testosterone-spiked buffet. Men are ever-present like Botox on a celebrity forehead. I find myself at events where I'm the only man, like I've snuck into a women-and-chil-dren-first lifeboat, and men are mere stage hands dressed in black shifting the scenery. I'm not suggesting the sexes should be separated, I'm not advocating dick-apartheid, but even the most female spaces – hen dos, baby showers, spa days, films where women are friends for a number of years sharing the trials and tribulations of daily life and that's the entire narrative – are male-adjacent too, whether it's a question of stags, impregnators or, well, the male skew of Hollywood. Weirdly the only other female-specific space I can think of right now is a Tupperware party and Lord knows men love moist leftovers.

I wish I could adopt the MDMA advice a high woman gave me in the loos at a party. 'Always dab, never snort' she said, but I have been snorting men my whole life, great piles of them like Scarface. I dabbled, only to become a high-functioning addict, and I have never successfully detoxed. I've never been able to clear my system. I am hooked. As I thumb-scroll my memories, I realise every moment intersects with masculinity in some way, either impacted by the actions of men, or causing a recalibration of my own sense of maleness. Some memories are more piercing and invasive than others. I lost my virginity on ecstasy to a short dick with the girth of a car battery. I woke up the next afternoon thinking 'what the fuck was that?'. And that's a reoccurring theme with men. To the pink towel guy, to bowling balls manspreader, to the overhead overlord: 'what the fuck was that?'. After I lost my virginity, I had been penetrated by masculine energy and, though it had undoubtedly altered my own masculine energy, I was none the wiser. You immediately know where you stand with an erection, don't you? It's right there, pointing at you, making a sort of solid sense, a hard truth. But after my sexual jump-start with a car battery dick, I was still all at sea. As a newly card-carrying homosexual, I was besotted with men. Okay I wasn't newly besotted with men themselves, but I'd had certain realisations about their capabilities and a newfound, more precise and localised interest in them. The way they moved. The way they acted. I was a sexual blank slate full of hope and desire and possibility. The men I met fucked it up royally.

I have met so many men that left me on edge, some of whom had the audacity to leave me on read. There have been more bad dates than a rotten sticky toffee pudding. There were the tight men who didn't buy me any drinks, or slyly ordered themselves doubles when I was a singleton. I once went on a date with a chap and he turned around at the bar mid-date and made out with someone else. I fled out into the night trying to sober up and bumped into them half an hour later coming out of the club when I returned for my coat. I thought I'd hit the jackpot with the Scottish, short, GSOH guy who knew how to drop an acerbic meme in the chat, but he was yet another boyish time-waster, whose main personality trait, when finally revealed, was being tired. I understand that being tired is a thing, that an aura of stress and typing stabby emails on your phone and doing big dramatic yawns when it goes quiet in a room is somebody's type of person, it's just not mine. In my early twenties, my sexual psyche couldn't resist men imported from Spain, which is at best a fetish, at worst low-level racism. A Spanish guy I worked with toyed with my emotions like my heart was one of many in the tapas of his potential conquests (I'm not certain it's okay to do a tapas metaphor, but here it is). Despite the Spaniard vaguely insinuating he wasn't interested, I felt like he was giving me signals, little clues that he liked me back, like when people see Jesus on slices of toast. I was addicted to the unrequited-ness. In fairness, he gave some quite explicit signals he was not down to fuck and my own denial gaslit me. It culminated one night with me drunk at a bar while Doris Day's 'Perhaps, Perhaps, Perhaps' played, singing 'If you can't make your mind up go back to Espania,/Cause I don't wanna wind up hasta manana'. This was, I'm ready to admit, a low point.

So, fuck – and I don't say it lightly – men. Fuck the toying Spaniards. Fuck the time-wasters. Fuck the *is this a date?* ers. I'm not sure I have ever been gaslit, because maybe the gaslighting was so good I didn't notice, but fuck the gaslighters. Fuck the cheapskates and fuck their single-measure drinks. Fuck enticing senses of humour and acerbic memes. Fuck pink towels. Fuck overhead baggage. And while you're at it, get your fucking knee off my sliver of fucking seat, close your fucking legs. Fuck phallic architecture. Fuck the Gherkin, and fuck every obelisk. Fuck Stonehenge, although maybe Stonehenge is okay? Fuck the Taj Mahal and the Eiffel Tower. Fuck Freud. Fuck Carl

Jung. And fuck Nietzsche, just because. Fuck Hollywood and stag dos and men dressed in black adjusting the world behind the scenes. If we're really going there, fuck the guy who said 'I'm being fucked by a huge black cock' just before he came, honestly, fuck him, and fuck his jelly shoes. Fuck the misogyny. Fuck the homophobia. Fuck the fucking patriarchy. Shrew me the hell up. Not to sound like that Meredith Brooks song but I'll be your bitch and I'll be your prude and you can fucking lump it. Fuck the chrysalis of masculinity that constrains everything we do. Fuck. Fucking. Men.

There's only one niggling, outstanding problem I have with this. One thing stopping me binning off men completely.

I am one.

Newquay

Due to unforeseen circumstances, and the continued scheduling conflict that is married life, I'm spending four nights on Crete completely alone like Shirley Valentine. I find myself at the beach, ordering gruesomely sweet frozen daiquiris and sending topless selfies to friends in rainy London. I have *The New Yorker* open on an article about cyber fraud so I will be thought of as intellectual by nearby loungers, but it's a cerebral smokescreen. My mind's actually engrossed in a podcast on what a guest would eat for their last meal. My death row meal, thanks for asking, will be three crème brûlées in appropriate course sizes – a savoury basil one to start (though I'm not sure the literal burnt sugar of a brûlée can be anything but sweet), a pizza-sized one as the main with a side of spinach to keep me regular, and something tiered to finish because why mess with a classic. I listen to Diane Morgan on the podcast as she selects breads and sides. No disrespect to the deadpan legend Diane, but she sounds like she's on the zillionth interview of a taxing press junket and has also never heard this podcast before she Zoomed in. She is staunchly refusing to order an imaginary starter or an imaginary pudding, as if the very concept of an imaginary restaurant where the menu is pure fantasy irks her.

Meanwhile, I'm surrounded by families, stripes of pale humans in umbrella shadow, flambéing their burnt skin with tanning oil. I'm wearing sunglasses, obviously, ostensibly to minimise glare, to ward off early-onset blindness and to avoid those squint wrinkles you get when you squint, but there's another bonus too – there's men everywhere and, well, nobody can see me glancing. I can look at the men, safely surveying the Speedoed gussets of European men, a breed that's never had the bandwidth for board shorts. I am in a sea of beach bulges, of smuggled budgies, of hammocked bananas. Bulges tell you everything and nothing about a man, their promise can be empty, more wish list than gift, more nutsack than sausage. But the mystery is the titillation here. All that brimming erection capability, but no actual erections. So much juice worth the squeeze, but I am juiceless, a casual observer, a key witness. This is not my first time casually perusing flaccid beach dick, nor, I suspect, will it be my last. Whether you embrace it or not, there's a sexuality to the beach, the most public setting with everyone in their most private clothing. Bikinis and Speedos are just water-optimised underwear, not even waterproof, but quick-drying pants that operate differently where the sea meets the sand. As beachgoers in garments that exactly match our underwear, we're somehow *not* people in our underwear. 'We're bathers,' we tell ourselves, 'we're tourists.'

The pound of flesh on show carries a different weight. The context is crucial.

And it's harmless, I think, all the communal covert looking, all my personal covert looking. The noticing, the appraisal, a benign reminder I still have some testosterone bubbling somewhere below the waist, gradually diluting since puberty of course, but still keeping me somewhat surveillant. I know I'll eventually reach an age where I have soft peaks instead of these nearly-pecs and my thinning virility will present as menacing (perhaps *sad* is the word?). I must savour my dwindling potency before I'm impotent, before I'm old enough that the stage-managed sagging can be seen from the gods. There's a certain unfair leeway for younger man to be gross, to ogle. Societally we cut a lot of slack for a chap in his early-prime when his hormones are still lairy. There's a leniency towards beach-staring if you have the newly-bubbling testosterone to back it up. A middle-aged man is less delicious, but still very much edible, so that passes too. But a gross old man gawping at young pouches is straight up wretched, a vulture eye-feasting on young flesh. I wonder at what age that balance tips from bulge appreciator to sand pervert, from cock connoisseur to creep? What is my stare-by date? Maybe I've already surpassed it? That simply doesn't bear thinking about.

And as I sit here I'm reminded of beaches past, the comic sands of my youth. But as my toes settle into my beach-combed memories, I'm slapped in the cerebral cortex by an absolutely miserable recollection. The vision comes to me like a suddenly inflating airbag in a traffic collision, suffo-cating me. It all happened one fateful night on the golden sands in Newquay, just below the hotel from *The Witches*, the summer I left school.

After a decent spread of GCSEs, I headed West with a bunch of plucky gal pals to celebrate not having to imme-diately apply for fast food jobs. We were like *Five Go Camping* with lashings of Lambrini instead of ginger beer. There were a lot of us, a group of sixteen rather than Blyton's famous quintet. To level with you, I'm not that versed in Blyton literature, but a good friend told me she's an alleged racist and whenever I hear her name my thoughts are pierced with the image of four golliwogs and a dog in a boat. My large circle of friends thankfully didn't mirror this scene. Some of them I was close to, lifelong best friends in the making, others were like a Christmas cousin you chat to animatedly on Boxing Day after three Baileys but would never be proper friends with in real life. We had spent the afternoon we got our GCSE results at the local park symbolically burning our homework diaries and signing each other's shirts with Berols. On some shirts I just wrote 'good luck', because I knew I'd never see the girl again, a premonition of a well-edited life, an amended social circle. There were people I deleted at sixth form, and even at my most socially vulnerable on my first day at university, I refused to lock onto anyone, knowing some of these new acquaintances would get abridged. This makes me sound like a cut-throat friend, the kind that would never suffer through a dead friendship, not even for the sake of prosperity, which I am. The worst friendships collide bi-annually, usually at a wedding or baby shower, and the only common ground is the past so it's all you talk about. There were fun times, when you were co-collaborators in fun, you were a team. But years pass and now one or more of you isn't fun, or cannot be fun because of an amassed responsibility, and you all kindly resort to reliving sixth form nights of hedonism, alongside veiled judgemental appraisals of your current lifestyles. Whether you're of the settled family camp, or still a wedding crasher, the grass is always greener and you have to act like your own decisions on the cragged route to happiness were the best ones. Women can smell judgement at fifty paces, but usually from other women so I go relatively unscathed. I always assume it's connected to some biological patter that happens between women when I'm out the room, some continual discussion of cycles and cramps and nipple sensitivity and bras and orgasms and, well, femininity itself. It's all part of this tapestry of female friendship that women never really stop stitching, connecting the bodily and the emotional. As a man with mainly female friends, I have a sort of hall pass for discussions of physicality, I'm expected to be sympathetic if downstairs mechanics aren't running completely smoothly, but I'm not expected to *understand*. Perhaps I could change it up? I wonder what would happen if, when sitting down to a nice risotto and a bottle of Chablis, I asked my mate about her vagina. 'How is your minge, darling, how are your nipples?'

It's not off limits as a topic, it's not taboo, but my female friends and I don't *go in*, we don't talk about their vaginas in the same way I don't explain to them how much I love, I dunno, having erections, maybe or, well, looking at bulges at the beach. It's no better or worse on the side-lines of femininity, it's just where I find myself. And that hall pass gets me out of other classes too. The greatest male privilege might be the ability to hang out with people you don't rate highly and them not having the slightest idea. Women don't watch you the way they watch other women, they don't scrutinise the micro-expressions, they don't have the same expectations. After the slightest, almost imperceptible glint of a female-to-female misdemeanour they might text 'why are you being weird with me?' to the offending party. Or 'was it me, or was she being weird with me?' to other members of the congregation, other seamstresses of that female tapestry. Pull one thread and the entire textile notices.

Anyway, I went to Newquay with my mates. Every so often, throughout my school days, someone would get rejected from the group, such is the savagery of teenage girl-dom. Newquay was, in a way, a victory lap for the social survivors, for the women still embroidering, who never missed a stitch. The sixteen of us didn't have a collective noun because in the time before WhatsApp groups, rather than 'Hannah's Hens' or 'Crete Lads', we were all just people. People in a nameless group. We did, however, have a united collective goal: Mike Skinner frivolity in cargo trousers and belly tops. We wore a lot of gold jewellery in an ironic townie way. We talked about clubbing, but only a handful of us had ever been inside a club. We talked about sex in similar terms. Looking old enough for either was social currency. We had emerged from childhoods – reared on Kellogg's Start (which didn't have a free toy), Ninja Turtle pizzas from Asda and the hidden sugar in Sunny Delight – and survived the civil war of Blur versus Oasis. Having lived through *My So-Called Life* and *The Miseducation of Lauryn Hill* we were emotionally-equipped, theoretically at least, for latter teenagerhood. This was our first holiday without adult supervision, eight Thelmas and eight Louises hitting the coast. We'd chosen the beaches of Newquay as our escape from the teenage rat race of sitting in the park reading magazines and learning to roll. Real jobs were a daydream, but I believe our collective career goal was modelling on the side of either *T4* presenter or part-time *Vice* Don'ts writer, or the person on the door of a club who decides who gets in – the perfect mix of well-dressed and judgemental.

Have you ever been sixteen? I'm assuming you have. Or maybe you're not sixteen yet and honestly, you've seen too much in this book for a child's eyes. But like any mid-teen, my personality was still forming like magma. I was Michelangelo clay waiting to become David. I wanted to be a conglomerate of influences – I wanted desperately to be associated with *The Face*, very nonchalant and spunky. I wanted to be the sexy boy from *Sexy Boy* by Air, beguiling with a dash of French *je ne sais quoi*. I wanted to be a character from *This Life* or *The Lakes*, more in attitude than low socioeconomic status. I also wanted to be like Samantha in *Sex and the City*, a woman who fucks a guy one summer because his family have a pool. The only gay culture I remember on the telly was *Queer as Folk*, with the virginal Nathan getting rimmed on a school night by Stuart. I didn't want to be either of them. From my lovers – lovers being nothing more than a hypothesis at this point – I wanted Jane Austen romance, heaving breasts under corsets, but my outer shell was Twisted Levis. I wanted men to fall completely in love with me, in an unhealthily obsessive way, those hearts round their heads like on Photo Booth, but I didn't want to be bogged down by my own emotions. I wanted to be footloose and fancy-free and infinitely fuckable. As men went head over heels, I wanted to remain a calm, mysterious *je ne sais quoi* sexy boy, inoculated against heartache.

At this exact time, a recurring life theme was beginning to take effect: an insatiable desire for personal tales of adventure. As a nascent party monster, I was always getting things wrong, always fucking up, but my modus operandi was to transform those benign catastrophes of youth into witty two-liners, the perfect pub banter. I wanted to be able to retell my misdemeanour stories that made people both wince and laugh, so I neatly packaged every calamity from every night out into excruciatingly captivating vignettes. To date, *The Chronicles of Raven Smith* have included: falling in human shit at Gay Pride; the time a cloakroom attendant let us search the cloakroom for a lost coat and we 'found' a miniature bottle of clear Jack Daniels, downed it, and flew home off our tits, scribbling on each other's faces with a bingo marker; the party where the birthday girl took acid at 8 pm and refused to open presents because she was terrified of the wrapped boxes; the time I accidentally took two sleeping pills before work, trying to ward off an early hangover; the night at a pretentious artist's where we thawed and drank shots of his blood from the freezer. Sometimes I've torn someone's passport in half just because, sometimes I've encouraged everyone to stab the Habitat lampshades with kitchen knives like duelling cavaliers, sometimes we've snorted lines of cheap black pepper off the table at the all-night diner just to feel something, sometimes I've strained vodka from a chipped bottle through a pair of tights rather than bin it. We once found a huge block of ice on the way to a house party and gifted it to the host, only for all our drinks to taste of market fish. There was a sort of extreme bro culture at the time, of being a fucking ledge, which gained wider public consciousness via MTV's *Jackass*, but I don't think these tales of boozing are exclusive to turn-of-the-century Brighton. These stories, often involving but not exclusive to vomit and faeces, were part of a self-mythologising. A way to swagger through the chaos of late adolescence. A way to drink and be expressive and daring, without anyone cottoning on that you were sad. A smoke-screen for existential dread. In the same way Hans Christian

Andersen narratives are critiques of morality, the moral of these stories was always to show you're both up for anything, and impenetrable to embarrassment. You might think you're an ugly duckling, but nobody will notice when you're retelling the story of climbing up on a pub sink on New Year's Eve, it cracking in half, and the pub being evacuated hours before midnight. It's worth pointing out at this point that if your tales of drinking merely involve a rather long list of everything you drank one night and concludes with 'we were so drunk, tho', I don't really want to hear it, it echoes the baby shower chat that refuses to move us forward as a species because we're hellbent on looking back. Nobody cares that you had a skinful, my love, please regale the group with what you did with the residual booze energy, or kindly shut up.

This particular night in Newquay has yet to make it to the chronicles, because some things are too hard to laugh away and shrug off over a pint. Some shame is too deep to recondition as an anecdote of note, no matter how hard I try. I remember little from actually being in Newquay that celebratory GCSE week. My mind presents a few snapshots of boogie boarding and standing in the freezing cold one night waiting for the fire brigade's all clear after we took the casing off the fire alarm and blew smoke into the sensor 'to see what would happen'. I remember crashing another hostel and pushing the vending machine over and everyone eating Walkers Max as the sun came up. A guy proudly showed me a (physical, paper) picture of him losing his virginity to a prostitute. I remember wearing a black shirt and chain, which was off-brand, way too smart for a boy raised on Kellogg's Start, but seemed like the best way to get into the clubs. The Newquay clubs of summer 2000 were neon-ed to the point of nausea, their floors adhesive from too many spilled drinks. And it was in one of these clubs that I met a man.

I say man, but he was more of a boy, like myself, and barely out of short trousers. I remember nothing of his face. I assume I've blocked the trauma out like childbirth, an amnesia created by my brain to spare me harm. I do remember the migraine-inducing smell of his cheap aftershave, a miserable muskiness, thick as almond butter, which has haunted me henceforth. A man by any other name would smell as unsweet. He materialised from nowhere, and I was game. There was some frenzied snogging on the dance floor (just the right amount of awkward) and then we escaped to the beach, a place that only hours before had been awash with day-trippers in wetsuits and toddlers in armbands. His aftershave was not diluted by the sea breeze. In the darkness, it was actually intensified, overwhelming my nose like I'd snorted crushed-up bath bomb, and dulling my other senses. Despite the vicious nasal assault, we dry humped against some rocks, all drunk elbows and teenage thumbs, an embarrassment of hands, like shipwreck driftwood. We were lovers locked in a jagged embrace, the salt air whipping at our ears, but no Jane Austen affair was blooming under the stars.

The guy pawed at me. He wanted a rummage, a genital handscrabble. Yet I had never had a man at my crotch before. I'd had a couple of same-sex kisses already, which were almost the same as the girls I'd kissed but tasted less of The Body Shop. He was grappling for my downstairs and all I remember is a rising sense of fear that he would actually touch my penis. That I would somehow pass through a gateway, away from my teenage mutant ninja childhood and into the adult dimension, all dinner parties and VAT returns. It was thrilling in part, because my testicles were par-dropped and hormones were flooding my black-shirted frame. I had the motive, not the means for a handjob. Or perhaps the means, and not enough of a motive to fully surrender. I felt like Liesl von Trapp facing the world of men: innocent as a rose. So utterly timid and shy and scared was I, that rather than unzip my flies and let the adult world in, I panicked. I let the parallel lines of intrigue and fear conjoin at a stop sign. I bottled it. I felt the need to halt proceedings as soon as humanly possible, but without an adult's confidence to say no thank you out loud, I had no resources to press pause. I had only one avenue left to dart down, and I'm not proud that I took it. Like any good tale-chaser on a night out, I improvised. Reader, I pretended to cum in my pants.

We stumbled back to the club in silence. There's no deny-ing that this was a bad sexual experience, my worst to date. My body was effectively unharmed, but my ego was in bits and my nuts were starting to really hurt. I remember nothing more of the beach, my ability to make memories drowned out by the voice screaming 'what the fuck did you do that for?' in my head. Where do I even start on pretending to jizz yourself? Is it worse than actually jizzing yourself? There's nothing to mop up, which is the only silver lining in this whole teenage cream of a mess. Then again, it's perhaps worse to pretend to be a terrible shag, than actually be a terrible shag. To be a little boy who spaffs at the first sign of a palm might be less soul-destroying than my fake orgasmic performance. Being a terrible shag shows at best a certain willingness, the endeavour to shag at all, even if badly. I think about common sexual issues – getting hard, staying hard, the time in minutes you spend doing things that basically boil down to friction endurance. Nearly all of these involve the penis being *outside* the jeans, the hyphen at the end of a dick being *visible*. I had fallen at the first hurdle, before the pistol had gone off. Not even that. I had faked my own pistol's blast halfway through the warm up.

You might think in a book about men and our egos, this would a great time to get into the ins and outs of faking an orgasm. Though I'm keen for any men who've willingly faked it to please get in touch with me, anonymity guaranteed, fake orgasms feel majority female. In a way, I can see the appeal of making the man feel like he's done a good enough job, that he's got you so close to your finish line you pretend he's crossed it out of kindness, a bit like a treat for a dog you're training. But that's as far as I'll go in terms of why women fake, it's absolutely something to ask them. I'm not sure I have any expertise outside of this night on the beach, I'm uncertain I'm best placed to dissect the intricate minutiae of the subject.

In the cold light of present times, I simply cannot understand pretending to cum when you haven't cum, and as my portal to instant adulthood closed I couldn't understand it then either. I had styled myself as up for anything. I was looking at printed out pictures of real people having sex. As I post-rationalise my decision-making, I like to think of the whole situation as pure. Very innocuous and chaste and Jane Austen, though I don't remember any fake orgasms in *Pride and Prejudice*. Do we even know for sure that Mr Darcy never faked an orgasm? We all know I wouldn't be able to say if he'd already been in touch anonymously, I would protect my source. I'd love to offer some rationality to my actions but I struggle to really gain any understanding other than that I was just a kid. A kid with the emerging body of an adult, but still a kid. The main thrust of being sixteen is to prove your adulthood, to experience adult things and pretend to take them in your stride, to drink and smoke and finger like it's no big deal. I had been offered a big deal, and squandered the opportunity. This faked beachgasm was an innocent fumble, before my life got more complicated. Before I was tripped up by my own sense and sensibility. Before my foot was perennially in my mouth and my dick hyphen was outside my jeans.

I wonder, too, if the living cloud of aftershave even remembers the event? If he sometimes recalls the boy-man who creamed his boxers against a rock, at the beach below the hotel from *The Witches*? I wonder if I appear in his chronicles? Even as a side note? A scribble in the margin? With the ferocity of a mother lion protecting her young, I vow to never, ever find him and never, ever find out. An olive-skinned mate of mine did her genealogy thing and was so white she's regretted it ever since, she was hoping for the tiniest tabasco dash of something exotic but she got majority Norman. That would happen with the man candle, there would be no satisfactory resolution, only a second wave of disappointment. He could never find me anyway, I would smell him at fifty paces and scarper. My nose is ever vigilant to the pilot fish of his scent, I am the canary down the mine.

As I order a third frozen daiquiri in Crete, Speedoed men frolicking in the surf, waiting staff nodding intellectually at my *New Yorker*, I get the sinking feeling that if it were ever commissioned, my *Guardian Experience* would be pretending to cum in my pants on a rock in the West Country. I'm not sure what I learned about myself on the rocks. The resolve to not phantom cum in my knickers was instantaneous, and I've never done it again. But here it is, a tale I can finally bear to tell. Twenty years later, another chapter in *The Chronicles of Raven Smith*, 'The Night I Faked an Orgasm'.

The Ghost

I see the man that ghosted me and I immediately compose him an appropriate text: 'You look shorter in real life, are you still a cunt?'. We're in the street and he does look shorter, like when you see celebrities in the flesh, so it's a fair point. It's such an excellently crafted hyper-speed retort, such an act of instantaneous and layered passive aggression, I'm almost inclined to believe in God and believe that she's real. Divine intervention via written snapback. Okay, on the second read of the message I can see there's not huge quantities of passive in the passive aggressive. It's fully aggressive. Pit bull on heat aggressive. Penalty shootout aggressive. I delete the text so The Ghost can't see those three dots that say I'm typing.

Seeing him in the flesh is weird. It happens so quickly that I'm not even sure it's happening until I'm past him. I refuse to look back and check. Not for anything. Not for all the tea in China. I fight to control my neck muscles, to freeze them with the *Bernard's Watch* of my mind. It works. I don't look back. A tiny victory.

I'm transported back eighteen months, to a time when we were chatting online. Flirtatious, nonsexual chatter. I send him pictures of me in my pants, which I admit are not totally unsexual, but I've already posted them on Instagram so they don't feel like illicit transgressions. Nothing bespoke. Harmless. He gets in a bike accident and his face is all mashed up. When he sends me a selfie of his plum-bruised eye, I say he still looks cute. I say he still looks hot. We joke that I'm like the perverts in *Crash* who get off on traffic collisions. I say that sometimes when I'm horny I wander into the road in my pants hoping for a milk float and a hot milkman but I don't illustrate the point with a visual. I am being fucking charming and funny. I am pitch perfect. Me at my most adorably highfa-lutin. The neuroses dialled down, barely audible. I ask if he wants drinks, or dinner, or dick, and he Keyzer Sözes me. He's gone. Nothing.

I didn't get where I am today by taking no for an answer. I think of myself as a Michelle Obama type, knocking down doors. I text The Ghost over the next few months: 'What's up? How's tricks?' Nothing. Later, in an act of unparalleled weakness I say, 'I'm not completely sure what happened here, we really got on'. Nothing. The trail is cold.

I just checked the graveyard of those archived WhatsApp messages and The Ghost is *online* ... now. The fucking spec-tre. I didn't message him because I'm a big boy and the time for séances has well and truly passed. He's changed his profile picture to one of him on a boardwalk somewhere that could be the Maldives (?), but it doesn't look like a private swimming spot because there's two heads bobbing in the background water like seals. I feel relieved. It's probably a Thomson package deal. A Tui. There's no way The Ghost is haunting a private island, is there? I can't see his face because he's wearing a Ralph Lauren cap and holding a disposable camera to his eye, the analogue prick. There's a towel on his shoulders and he's wearing Speedos. I begrudgingly note his thighs. I screengrab the picture and send it to my mate with the caption 'The Ghost!'. He replies that guys who wear Speedos like that are sluts. I send my mate a picture of me in my Speedos. Don't worry, it's already been on Instagram.

You can maybe feel my obsession here. My morbid fascination. My inability to just leave it. My intense interest with a man who I was never *that* fussed about. That's what irks me the most. The way an only-okay guy has mildly-flattered his way into my brain territory, and managed to set up a quite a robust base camp by way of total inaction. I can reconcile being blanked by someone who's better than me. I understand natural selection and that the hyper-hot must move from man to man like bees pollinating flowers. That is their calling. But The Ghost wasn't hyper-hot. He was the one reaching. I was the funny charming one, he was the dyspraxic cyclist. I was never envisioning some beautiful sun-dappled future, at most this was a *Crash* shag with a not-that-hot milkman. He was only ever so-so. He was never The One, but he became The Something. Now he's The Ghost, capitalised. He's set up camp in my brain like those irritating Burning Man hippies. He's a pebble in my beach sandal. A scratchy label on a T-shirt. A stain on my memory, like Bill on Lewinsky's dress. I want to Cillit Bang this man, to sponge him from my head.

There's one thing that strikes hard to the heart of any extrovert: a deletion of attention.

The audacity of it. The gall. The balls to ignore Raven Smith. I note the sliver of respect I have for his chutzpah. The Braveheart bravery. A resentful regard for his commitment to supernatural disappearance. But I pride myself on my banter, my ability to get on with people, so this all feels like a slight. A critique of my personality. And not even my whole character, the early doors, the previews before the film. He didn't like the temperature of my temperament. It's not the intricate pain of a breakup, that feeling that someone who knows you has opted out based on a rational series of decisions. I'd respect that. I'd stop and chat to my ex because at least he gave it a chance, at least he rolled the dice. It's the denial of possibility. This person doesn't believe in my potential. Or can't see it. It's like a job interview where you don't really want the job but you want the job to want you. But being ghosted doesn't so much play into my insecurities as awaken my seething rage. Rage is like a lukewarm buffet, it's always there, gently heated, ready to be portioned out. Being ghosted makes me angry because it's another door closing, damming the ever-expanding pool of possibility, and I have zero say in the outcome. The Ghost took the power when he left me on read. I don't want vengeance. I want my control back.

Ghosting is shit. There's enough essays on that. A friend of mine with a Northern accent (why do Northern accents always feel so pragmatic? Is it the way they pronounce *sure* with two syllables?) says 'I don't get the issue with ghosting, if a guy doesn't like you, just move on'. It's a fair point. Why invest in a bank with a vault that never opens and all the cashpoints are hidden? Why roulette? I want to be the person who just moves on. Who walks down an avenue of ghosts as fearlessly as Yvette Fielding on *Most Haunted*. But also I want my upper hand back.

I want to think that The Ghost turned around and saw the back of my beautiful head, and realised how great I am (without ever seeing those three typing dots). I want him to have a personal epiphany in the street, like he's listening to a podcast and nodding furiously. I want him to think he's fucked it up, to lament our banter, our nascent embryo of something, and I want him to think that I categorically don't care. Because I'm flawed and fallible, I want him to think about me, but I want him to only remember that I'm funny. He'll imagine me composing him savage texts that emasculate him by inferring he's short, but I won't do that. He'll imagine I still think of him, but I won't. He'll imagine I write essays about him, but I won't.

The Second Taste
of Blackcurrant

The first time I got properly drunk I got punched in the head. I'd never really drunk before, just the dregs of cans of cider bequeathed to me by slightly scary middle-class girls in combat trousers, while Baz Lurhmann's *Romeo + Juliet* soundtrack played, in a kitchen of someone whose parents were away for the weekend. My parents, when at home and hoping, I assume, to de-fetishise my manic obsession with adult pursuits (drinking; smoking; I think they thought I was shagging, too), had allowed me to dip an anointed toe into the holy wine on sacred weeknights. A glass of white as dinner simmered, a shandy at the pub on Boxing Day, letting me try my first champagne like Liesel von Trapp at a wedding. I wasn't allowed the big-hitters of spirits (an attempt to order a vodka coke at a theatre bar during an interval was swiftly thwarted) but I knew almost immediately, beyond a shadow of a doubt, that with booze, I was onto a winner. Those early sips were transformative, a game for the senses when the alcohol hit my bloodstream, expedited by my teenage metabolism. I could see no drawbacks to boozing, partly because my medicine had been carefully rationed by consenting adults, and partly because I'd never had a hangover (latter years would find me panic-downing two Yakults on the way to uni, trying to steer the toxins of my body onto a soberer course). Drinking was like slipping into a personally-tailored jacket made of buttery calfskin, familiar and reassuring. I was a flower leaning towards the sun. Despite being a tall, I felt taller. I was more resilient, I was more resourceful, I was more fun. I felt more confident, which is an easy transition when you're an awkward teen (there's no other type of teen). I felt like Columbus cruising into new waters, a deck of at ease sailors entering a brave new world where your personality sparkled like wine. Having supped from the sweet teat of my better, unsober self, I had been left with a taste for more. I had the exciting anticipation of full frontal drunkenness, an ambient sense of willing but hadn't witnessed the full thing.

The full thing was horrific. Last day of term, Year 8 I think. It must have been Year 8 because it was the last day of Year 9 that I got suspended for cutting my school trousers into shorts. I was a committed seamstress: I'd spent an evening snipping and hemming the trousers, rather than just rolling them up. I had such a toxic relationship with my Home Economics teacher – a nutty woman that grew up in the Welsh Valleys and claimed she'd never seen a pepper until she went to university (!?) – that the neat hemming of the school slacks served as an accomplished retaliation to the lacklustre way I'd approached her classes (she actually took me to one side and made me promise not to take

Home Economics at GCSE). The new shorts I'd made got me booted out of school in first period. I had an IT lesson but my rather vigilant Geography teacher, who was known for his massive calves and willingness to do drag for the school panto, took the class, saw the shorts and marched me to the front office. I was back on the mean streets of rural Lewes before 9.30 am; I had fallen at the first hurdle.

Anyway, the finale of Year 8: summer was upon us and the air smelled of Lynx Africa and Vanilla Kisses. We were all high on the Quaalude that is no school for six weeks, but that wasn't enough, we wanted to up the ante, to gild the lily: we wanted, above all else, to drink. Before going to the park (the only place teens are allowed to mingle for more than twenty minutes before getting moved on), I'd poured half a finger of every spirit in my parents' liquor cupboard into a Fanta bottle, topped with something blackcurrant-y to disguise the alcoholic taste. I then replaced each spirit with half a finger of water and honestly thought I was the most cunning master of deception known to man, like Fantastic Mr Fox versus Boggis and Bunce and Bean. I didn't skate, and yet I was dressing at the time almost exclusively as a skater. This was a time when the sixties were having a nineties moment and everyone worth their salt had an inflatable plastic chair. The look was 'Don't Speak', so bindis were huge too, cultural appropriation being a problem in the very distant future.

We met in the park and I drank the berry elixir in the park and I was suitably drunk in the park. I remember that quite clearly. Not trashy or deranged. Walking in straight lines still. Drunk for the first time and fucking loving every minute of it. The big end of year party was the following day, in a field with a caravan far away enough from parental supervision, and we still needed to get booze for that. Asking a legal drinker to buy you alcohol was (and perhaps still is) the best strategy for thirteen-year-olds searching for alcopops like pigs for truffles. A kind soul passing the Oddbins we were stationed at, high on either the weather or the potency of our collective Lynx Africa, took pity on us and agreed to buy us a litre of vodka. A litre of vodka. Between two people, sure, but a litre of vodka. The rest, quite understandably, is merely remembered in snapshots.

The park again. The hot day, the hot grass. The vodka bottle empty (how?). The sweet, euphoric emptying of the bladder, a torrential release of urine behind a bush. Trying incredibly hard to concentrate on conversations. Trying to join conversations and people looking at me like I was speaking in tongues (I may have been), watching me with the kind of full-body alertness you do when unhinged people come at you in the street. Feeling an acute awareness of the dripping, unstoppable, dreadful futility of all things. Wave after wave of no return. Wanting to go back, back in time, back to Oddbins, back to school, back to long trousers, back to sobriety. My shoes feeling huge and soft. My T-shirt feeling thin and airless. The buttery calfskin jacket of drink closing around my chest, impossible to unzip and shrug off. Bindis swirling before my eyes. Overhearing someone saying 'Raven's definitely going to be sick later'. Repeatedly saying I wasn't going to be sick. The night finally closing in. The disorientation of the darkness. Checking my cargo trouser pockets (not sure what for). Taking another piss. Talk of another park, another spot where other teenagers weren't being asked to move on. Walking towards the other park. Not walking in straight lines now, but those drawn in vodka. My legs having rickets, my walking trajectory equally bowed. Getting to the other park.

Out of nowhere someone punching my head from behind (ah, the chivalry of teenage boys). Falling down and feeling more surprised than hurt. Getting up to run away and making it maybe two paces before falling again. The split-test of seconds with too much happening for me to react to. Somehow I was no longer being punched. Somehow I was sitting on a bench. Somebody was hiding me, sitting on my lap to shield me from the punchers who were just walking round the park at night looking for people to punch. Boys from my school. I remember crying, from shock and vodka, and saying 'everybody hates me' (not untrue). Then the vomiting. The vomiting. The vomiting. I was very, very sick in a garden of eternal rest off to the side of the second park. Crouched and feral and straining. The second taste of blackcurrant, remixed in hell itself. Revisiting each half-finger of my parents' liquor cabinet. The mouth vomiting. The nose vomiting. The sensory overload. The fear I was suffocating because I couldn't breathe in during the evacuation. The endorphins released when I realised I wasn't suffocating, that I wasn't dying. A lapse in vomiting. A rather weedy boy who was really into nerd things, very kindly asking me if I was okay (I was not). Someone helping me back onto a bench. Somehow at the train station (timeframes are in the bin at this point). Being on the train home and being comatose but not at all in a coma, and hearing a woman telling whoever was looking after me (honestly no idea who) to keep giving me water. Saying 'I'm fine, I'm fine' with my eyes completely clamped shut. Not drinking water. Somehow walking back to my house. Realising I didn't have keys (fuck you, cargo trousers) and sitting on the window sill. Within minutes my mum appearing, a celestial being materialising further up the street (it felt like minutes but it could have been six months, frankly). My guardian angel asking me how much I'd had to drink before putting me to bed. Finally drinking water. I drifted off to the sound of her on the phone saying 'he said a litre of vodka'. That's about it memory-wise. There's an incredibly vague idea, almost a mirage, of my mum making sure I wasn't in a coma at one or several points throughout the night. What a legend.

I still, to this day, have no idea who punched me. No cuts, no bruises, my keys were in the house where I'd left them. My mum took me to the Waffle House for lunch the next day and I went to that party that night and someone said 'apparently, you tried to run away and just fell over'. This was a girl who used to drink so quickly that rather than seem drunk or inebriated, she would just explode with vomit as her body rejected the assault. I was now a few rungs below exploding vomit girl on the party hierarchy. In fairness, I *had* fallen straight over, and I have no idea how many people saw.

That was my first foray into the land of the drunk. My parents, to their credit (either because they were carefully tenacious or plain stupid), still supported me drinking responsibly, coming back from France later that summer with a crate of bottled beers but rationing them to two-a-day like it was the Blitz. You'd think because of the adolescent hammering to the bonce, the cranial drumming, the bludgeoning by way of other teens, that I'd learned a lesson, that there'd be some kind of learning experience. You'd think I'd have connected over-drinking with a lack of adequate personal security. The utter unsafety of it all terrifies me now, not so much not having my wits about me, but leaving them in a park at night and zigzagging into danger. But I drank again, dear reader. As soon as the taste of blackcurrant stopped making me gag, I drank on. I drank on for years.

New York

I want to start this chapter with a warning: I do not advise drinking piss or taking Ritalin, it's a spell for disaster that I once cast on a winter's night somewhere over the East River in New York.

I'm abroad with my laptop and a bunch of feelings, thinking of my beloved London. Like a benevolent aunt, London has always been good to me, offering a sort of shit-caked glamour, an orphan grittiness, a Zadie Smith liberalness. I am a London jingoist. A city compatriot. I simply cannot get enough of the sprawling metropolis. The London you see in Channel 4 dramas, all council estates and hardened single mums, is a bit like the cobbled provincial north you see on Film4. There's a truth to the depiction, but that's not the whole story. We have Dickensian streets and Ottolenghis. Snaking queues in Soho for no-reservation restaurants. Hoards of knickerless revellers lemming-ed into smoking pens. We have a ton of Banskys to remind us we're artisanal and urban, and the Princess Diana fountain as a reminder of the pressures of royalty. There are the obligatory midriffs of Notting Hill Carnival and as many Sainsbury's Bag for Lifes as you can steal without scanning at the checkout. The rental market in London is a mess of course, but there was, and still is, plenty of spacious accommodation for people who hate their money. Estate agents will happily show you round a shoebox, whilst reminding you that you're a stone's throw from cosmopolitan Brick Lane, though my friend once bit into a sandwich there and lost a tooth to a large shard of safety glass.

I Dick Whittington-ed to London in the year of our Lord two thousand and three. When I first moved, there was a wild rumour about a secret bar where the boys walked on their hands and served drinks out of their arseholes through straws (I never found it). In Brighton, I had felt like an incredibly large fish in a small pond, outgrowing my aquarium and wanting to free my willy. It was time for me to live the reality of not having someone doing a big shop and refilling the fridge, of the inconvenience of unassisted survival. Despite fables of acrimonious Londoners with their brutal detachment disorders, the city life didn't faze me particularly. My story followed the narrative arc of every annoying romcom: small town girl finds herself in the big city, surrounded by a gaggle of multicultural friends. I jenga-ed acquaintances. I found a little clique. And I loved the city's anonymity: the faceless, eyes-down tube patrons; the women in commute-trainers; night buses Jackson Pollock-ed in puddles of alcoholic sick; the coffees from gormless baristas who misspelled your name; the macro-aggressions; the miscellany; the men. I passed bus stops I'd never thrown up at. I breakfasted at Percy Ingle. I bought enlarged kid's plimsolls in a side street. I Artful Dodger-ed. I Bridget Jones-ed across London Bridge in light snow, smiling my chubby cheeks off. I felt plucked from Brighton obscurity like an X Factor contestant. I was still obscure, but I was making it my own.

My first year at university was a belle époque, and *privilege klaxon* my mum paid my rent during term time. I realised I could live in relative comfort off my student loan if I drank 19p cans of cider before going out. Like all first years, my understanding of nutrition was shaky, but I knew enough to remain undead. Each day, I drank a litre of pineapple juice from the corner shop for the good of my health. Of course, I went out a lot. There were legendary house parties. Everyone remembers a legendary house party but I went to one every week and I only have three that stick out in my mind because house parties are like princes, you have to kiss a lot of frogs. You have to survive a lot of crappy kitchens in Acton with three horny mathematics students before you end up off your face at 5 am on a canal boat dressed as a pirate with the police instructing you to return the life ring round your neck to the glass case. There was a Halloween I dressed as Charlie Chaplin with centre-parted hair, which read from afar as Black Hitler. Halloween was always tricky if you are non-white because of the rather small pool of non-white celebrities, at least in 2006. The worst Halloween costume is 'some blood' but at least it's not racial. There was the time I left a party and got Morse code diarrhoea under a tree in Hyde Park, quite a long broadcast of dots and dashes. There was the time I fell off a table and into an oven (quite a feat).

By my third year at university I was living alone and going out every night. I remember maybe two nights in my flat in six months. At the same time I was ostriching my education, bunking lectures and delivering coursework at the last minute. In a way, with graduation looming, I was ostriching my future. I had a feeling the silliness of my childhood was ending, my life inevitably slowing to a crawl, to an official adulthood with nobody paying my rent. I wanted my adult life on the backbench, to run away from grown-up commitment like Billie and Chris's fuck-it marriage. I don't remember wanting any kind of career at this point, understanding that you either die a hero or live long enough to see yourself become the civilian. I had a dream of being a night crawler. I remember vividly coming home one weekend and earnestly explaining to my mum that I wanted to be a man about town. As a job.

My life at the time was measured in parties, but I had a wandering eye. London was my mistress until I cheated on her, embarking on a ninety-day affair with New York, the exact length of a tourist visa. I booked a flight to JFK three months after my degree, undercoating adulthood with one last hurrah. I say after my degree, but I'd actually failed to graduate because of some coursework I couldn't be arsed to do. This had meant that when I turned up on 'graduation' day, I had to sit in the audience with my mum in my full graduation gown. Imagine if you will a sea of proud, middle-aged parents and me in a square hat. After the ceremony, my graduating peer passed me her diploma and me and my mum did pictures with it. I was hideously hungover because I'd been to a dinner the night before and it was a bit boring so I put vodka in my white wine. I hadn't left until 9 am, when I'd sat bolt upright on the sofa and said 'I'm fucking graduating today'. I also didn't realise that you can see a person's clothes under the graduation gown so I was wearing a nasty striped H&M T-shirt that someone had left drying at the party that I'd just put on as I left. Anyway, it was about time to leave the country.

General adulthood wasn't the only thing I was escaping. I was struggling through the collateral damage of that first breakup and the funeral for a family friend, a girl my age with cystic fibrosis. She was always poorly in our childhoods, chuffing on an inhaler, but she got critically sick critically fast. I visited her in hospital but rather than be sad, rather than holding her hand and saying something meaningful, a comedian's patter poured out of me. I told witty anecdotes that eased everybody's pain, or at least deflected my own. There's a sort of irony in the transplant world in that you have to be very, very gravely ill to warrant a lung transplant, and within days you're too ill to accept the lungs. My mate didn't make it. Her window was too small for an appropriate donor. I remember sobbing into my stepdad's armpit to 'Reach for the Stars' by S Club 7 at the funeral, probably hungover. I remember her other friends had 'blinged-up' her casket with plastic decorations, which I thought was naff but made me cry even harder. I was a wreck. My parents were rightly worried about me, I was devastated and drinking heavily and moving to New York with nowhere to stay. I got the train back to London and went straight out that night, I remember wearing an electric blue string vest from Ridley Road Market and a wicker hat, my eyes puffed from crying. I had an emotional intelligence that felt like a curse, a challenge to the good times to be had, a party passion-killer, so I suppressed it. It wasn't super-cool to talk about your non-positive feelings in 2006, to be really fucking sad, to cry in clubs the day of a funeral. To survive, I became a mechanical pencil, soft graphite encased in metal. Metallics were in so nobody batted an eyelid.

I had this ebbing sense that my life was going the wrong way, my development not so much arrested as in full retrograde, like reading a self-help book backwards. Things were becoming more fraught, less evolved. People were getting entry-level jobs and I was back in the cave trying to make a fire with two sticks. But I escaped my regression, or at least put it on hold, and away I flew. I watched *The Devil Wears Prada* on the plane and I was very taken with the idea of scooting round NYC on a deadline in *the* Prada boots, and working for a hard-ass boss with a soft centre. A week before my flight, I'd randomly met a Manhattan-dwelling Brit at a lock-in who said I could sleep on his sofa when I arrived as long as I didn't tell immigration his name. I slept in a single bed under a mezzanine in a Tribeca loft for a month. I was a deliberate non-tourist. I've still never been to Katz's Deli, famous for serving fake orgasms. Instead, I walked down Fifth Avenue listening to 'Englishman in New York' on status symbol iPod headphones (white, long-wired). I was a lab rat of Limewire, I stole songs, a dandy highwayman of mp4s. I ordered bottomless coffee in diners. I liked my toast done on one side. I went to the Sunshine cinema. There was a Lagerfeld x H&M wedding dress collab and I went to see the hordes of tourists queueing round the block for Lily Allen tulle. I went on the giant *Big* keyboard at FAO Schwartz (that's a bit touristy). I drank PBRs at lesbian karaoke nights where some terribly sad looking girl would always sing Lisa Loeb's 'Stay' with the passion of the Christ.

My clothes were … interesting. Nobody really dresses for mood, do they? We project. We role play the life we really want. A great performance. Dressing for the promotion we covet at work, and the weather we'd prefer. Dressing like your usual self but on a day you had a savoury breakfast and haven't smoked a cigarette yet. Dressing like you've never been in the *Daily Mail*. Dressing like the kind of person who doesn't even look at the check before throwing down an AmEx. I dressed like the Artful Dodger had moved to New York, an unappetising garment salad. I wore the most aggressively look-at-me-living-my-best-life-on-a-tiny-budget clothing. I was already addicted to British charity shopping, visiting seaside towns for gems, but in New York I got to call it thrifting. I'd scavenge musty stores for 'finds' with the same fevered excitement as visiting the leisure centre vending machine after swimming. Because of my legs-up-to-the armpits and ski-flat feet, waist-down I'd dress exclusively from the high street. Converse were obligatory. Further up, my look was the tightest Topshop skinny jeans (that I took in further at the ankles) and dead men's shirts in garish patterns (that I took in so they were skin tight). I was smart-adjacent dressing – dress shirts, trench coats – but everything was threadbare or mothy. I wore a bowler hat. I found a gold raincoat and took it in on a sewing machine which compromised its waterproof-ability. Jewellery-wise, I had a penchant for bric-a-brac albatrossed at the neck, lassoed onto a chain with a spiral keyring. Anything metallic and not too weighty was slung against my chest. The bottom of a wrestling trophy. A camel from a nativity scene. Forgotten Christmas ornaments. The Artful Dodger in me was thriving, knowing you've got to pick a locket or two. I vividly remember my signature peanut-cum-tiny-knife hitting my ribcage as I bopped to 'Hounds of Love' (not the Kate Bush version).

Being British in New York is its own personality. Britishness makes you shiny like a tuppence. People think you're special. The novelty of it is crack for non-native Americans whose history started in like 1800. It's connected to our British royalty I think. Some properness imbued in the accent, with the idea that our women don't fall out of nightclubs, they curtsey and have tell-tale inflections of polite speech. Brits have the great ceremony of a shooting weekend, Americans have concealed amendment handguns. Realising the street value of my Britishness, I immediately became more pronounced in my English. I started pronouncing the L in almond. I sometimes said guv'nor. I sometimes said spiv. As I mentioned, I wore a bowler hat. I was the sort of whimsically charismatic Brit (read: stupid idiot) who leaves a nightclub at 3 am and crawls onto a bus to Philly.

Britney was off the rails in LA, driving erratically as her family googled conservatorships, but she was an amateur compared to the night dementors of New York, who dressed in head-to-toe deep-space black like vampire Ramones. The look was genuinely haunted Victorian doll. Club kids ruled the night. There were the people you'd see out drinking all the time: they had stupid hair and stupid nicknames that only you and your friends knew and shared privately. We had 'Brothers and Sisters', a family whose generational makeup didn't quite add up because they were a mother and her sons; 'Petito', who looked like a petit potato; does the nickname 'Skull in a Wig' need explaining? At one point I wanted to rebrand myself as 'Bobby London' ('Bobby' as in an English policeman), just to compact the Britishness. As I happily supplanted the East London hipsters for Brooklyn ones, I'd log into MySpace in the morning from my laptop and see if my outfits had worked and someone had taken any pictures of me at the party. The dream was a Cobrasnake shot, papped in the basement of Misshapes. My MySpace name was Raven Does Boys, but I was perennially single. I don't recall doing any boys, or vice versa.

No matter how hard you party, there's always someone partying harder. For the most part, I was partying harder than Britney. This was off the back of Britain's single flying-ants summer of new rave. New rave was like regular rave from the nineties, but newer, born in Hoxton and from what I remember very highlighter colours, very DIY. The music was synth-y (if music's your thing, you probably have a better take on the sound of that summer, I just remember gurn-dancing to Klaxons). From the inside, new rave never felt like a fad despite its garish aesthetic. Everyone had glow sticks and dummies and I was slowly transitioning from patterned cadaver shirts to Jeremy Scott sweats and check-erboard jeans from Trash and Vaudeville. Misshapes was still a thing, but the vampires had swapped their capes for klaxons, their vinyl for cassette playas. New York is fabled for its extreme seasons, but I don't remember any weather. I remember an assembly of the kind of hangovers when you look down at lunchtime and realise you're dressed as a fluo-rescent jester, or one of those Covent Garden street performers. I once pinned a black bow tie on an American Apparel vest (you have to say tank in the States) and wore it with green jeans, and nobody even blinked. There were no Sweetgreens back then, so in the daylight hours between Lower East Side jaunts, I lived off Starbucks frappes and single servings of Tropicana, the one with pulp left in for the sake of my health. I couldn't stop drinking gallons of Vitamin Water, the pink one affiliated with 50 Cent. I was experiencing Victorian consumption by way of a sugar overload. By the end of my trip I was drinking Sparks, which is basically a house party cocktail of caffeine and rubbing alcohol. The design of the can is a battery, indicating its ability to charge you up.

After a month in New York, I moved into McKibben lofts, a huge abandoned factory in the medium-bad part of Brooklyn. The building had a freight lift that we only used when visitors came to exemplify our new New Yorkness, and was a far cry from the *Rosemary's Baby*-type Upper East Side apartment I still dream of. The area is beyond gentrified now, you can't move for microbreweries, but at the time we'd hear gunshots and just shrug until a local resident said 'If you hear gunshots, you eat the fucking pavement'. McKibben smelled like teen spirit, but everyone was at least twenty-five with the faraway never-grow-up stare of Never Neverland Lost Boys. It was a tessellation of dorms, each containing up to six eccentric roommates that rarely had anything in common. My roomies were like a gnarled video tape of *Friends* where all the cast are distorted. Hester, a space cadet in the truest sense of the word, actually dressed as a space cadet, painted bright blue, for an alternative beauty pageant. My other flatmate had a dog called Vlad who remains the ugliest animal I've ever encountered, a sweet potato with four legs and bad breath. My upstairs neighbour Fahj remains a good friend. I met him on the steps of McKibben on Halloween and asked who he was dressing as. He said 'Kelly, Shoes' which will carbon date this period for some people. He went on to be McKibben's longest serving party boy, a veteran of the scene, advising over-partied youngsters like the Gamesmaster. The factory was a conveyor belt of merrymakings, you could always hear the beat of a good time calling out to you.

I grew accustomed to a life on the L train, visiting Manhattan for parties. I frequented go-go bars with open bars. I spent Halloween as the Jolly Green Giant, but we accidentally went to a club where a margarita was $20. I ate sweet potatoes topped with sweet marshmallows on Thanksgiving and drank more Sparks. One of my mates came out for a flying visit and we met under the lobster in Times Square. We got caught bunking the subway by the police and were issued official looking tickets that we still haven't paid. We took fake police mugshots on the platform, and in the freight lift up to the apartment she genuinely asked me if I was missing my pineapple juice (I was). I had, I noted, arrived at the authentic New York experience I was craving at twenty-one.

And then I met a boy.

He was a musician. Well, a performer. Well, a white rapper. An openly gay Eminem. His band were pretty good. The Musician (I'll call him that even though it conjures an erroneous image of a swaggering guy in leather, a vampire Ramone) was a new rave darling who wore patterned leggings unironically. I'd go to his gigs (again, that sounds quite rock'n'roll, which it wasn't). We'd eat grilled cheese at his place at 5 am, that he'd have to order because no takeaway people in Brooklyn can understand a

British accent laced with booze. He was confused if I was a top or a bottom and I honestly wasn't sure at that point. He really, and I don't say this lightly, liked to party. He never spent an evening at home. Ever. His entire schedule was slotting work around parties. He partied harder than me, who was partying harder than Britney. But while my Brit(ney) Abroad shtick was just an excuse for obnoxious vodka-ing, it was a chapter that I knew would close after ninety days. I was going hard and then I was going home. I was on a very long holiday, but a holiday it was. I had adulthood waiting for me back in London. For The Musician, this party was eternal. I don't care for the ins and outs of how we got together, but I was homesick in a way that I could feel in my bones. I was all at sea and drinking through it, tipping a dollar a drink to stave off the dread, the residual but-she-didn't-get-a-lung-transplant grief. Have you ever fallen in love with someone you shouldn't have fallen in love with? I've known a lot of men. I've slept with a handful. And nothing feels as acute as a chaotic romance when you're away from home, miles from familiarity. I always thought I was terrible at love when I was younger, that I sacrificed the wrong things and I stayed in bad relationships. But this one was a charade, a shimmer of the love I needed. I had a great big space ready to fill with another person but mine and The Musician's parts didn't quite fit. I had a longing for someone to caulk my cracks. It wasn't him, he wasn't the filler, but he was right there, and I could hold off on feeling sad a little longer. It's a rite of post-adolescent passage, I think, to neatly parcel up your heart and give it to someone with butterfingers. I think The Musician was simply too high to adequately hold onto it. I'm relieved, in retrospect, that it didn't tip into anything serious.

I don't remember how The Musician and I ended up at yet another afterparty in a loft on Christmas Eve Eve. My mum had arrived in late December in her huge red fake fur Monsoon coat (one that me and my mate had climbed into when we were stoned teens and accidentally torn the lining out of). She'd been with me for three nights, staying in Times Square which in retrospect seems quite flashy, and I took the opportunity to finally tourist New York – Rockefeller tree, Empire State building, that *Big* piano again, still no Katz's Deli. I'd packed her onto the plane home and naturally gone straight out. All I remember about the afterparty with The Musician is that the space was so huge that they had propped up a small boat and were using it as shelving, and the music was shit. Nobody was guarding the bottle of Patron on the giant kitchen island (more of a kitchen continent) so we took it. Straight into one of our thrifted coats it went and we left. We were halfway across the Brooklyn Bridge and several gulps down when I realised it was a bottle of lukewarm house party piss.

'It's piss', I said.

'It is not piss', he said.

This went back and forth with tentative re-tastes for

double-checking the piss by volume like grim sex party sommeliers. We made it perhaps another inch down the bottle before I noticed his giant pupils.

'You are on drugs,' I said, 'you are on fucking drugs. When did you get drugs you fucking drug addict? I cannot believe you're on drugs.'

I don't know if you know the mechanics of Ritalin? It's ADHD medication that makes you concentrate really fucking hard. A Canadian friend of mine, versed in the medicinal advantages of study drugs, had said it's fine to do if you're studying because you lock onto the paper that's due and don't look away. What you have to be careful of, she said, is what you lock onto, lest you spend the evening fixatedly stroking a cheese plant. I can appreciate, in retrospect, that if you're with someone on Ritalin and you say 'you're a drug addict, you're a drug addict' as you speed across the East River in the dead of night, all piss-drinking aside, they might be chemically susceptible to lock onto that. To become fixated on their own drug-taking. To question whether it's possibly tipping into addiction. We got home and I thought nothing more of it. I was annoyed I wasn't on drugs, I was annoyed I'd accidentally drunk piss. His pupils were black side plates at Nobu. I went to bed. It was a railroad apartment that only a week before had seen me walking in on his flatmate taking a dump.

He woke me early, gently stroking my head, to explain that I was right. That he was a drug addict. I didn't feel vindicated so much as half asleep. He then explained that he hadn't been to sleep at all, not one wink. Rather than sleep he had spent the whole night ringing everybody in his phone book to let them know he was a drug addict. His bandmates. His friends. My friend from under the lobster (Lord knows how he got her number). He'd called his mum and his stepdad. He'd called his father. This was, of course, without a shadow of a doubt, a bad thing. In the scheme of bad things, this was a really, really bad thing. High-dialling all your contacts to admit hyper-partying. Dream Phone, but a nightmare. He was leaving for home that afternoon anyway, because it was Christmas fucking Eve. All I could think was *this is the single most worst thing that could have happened while I slept*. What I actually said was 'try not to worry about it, it will all be fine'. Then I left. I didn't text him because texts from English phones to New York phones cost 60p for the sender.

Christmas came and went. I wanted to rent a room at the Plaza like Kevin McCallister, but couldn't afford it. Me and my housemate Tiny Tims stayed in the apartment in red union suits, listening repeatedly to 'All I Want for Christmas'. I had eggnog for the first time which is only one level above Sparks. Boxing day is a working day in America, who'd have thought it? Christmas night is essentially a school night. I saw The Musician again one last time and I don't remember once talking about the drug addict dial-a-thon. It was just too huge to chat through and I was leaving imminently. We had goodbye sex and he cried as he left McKibben afterwards.

Should I have done more? It wasn't a serious relationship. I wasn't staying. He was definitely fucking other guys. This was not serious. This was not *Homeo and Juliet*. This was a holiday fling. But should I have done more? He never asked explicitly for help. This felt like a Ritalin episode, rather than a drug addict reckoning. This wasn't a great love affair. It was the smallest of dalliances. It was two lost boys, escaping themselves, and trying to find a way home. Drug taking offers an escape of sorts from the status quo. If you're high enough you don't have to question how happy you are. Drugs numb you, that's what makes them so moreish. I want to say something serious, like 'I wasn't able to absorb The Musician's heaviness alongside my own, because I was too sad myself', but actually I was just twenty-one on holiday and a bit of an idiot, keen to bypass anything too serious.

New Year's was the big send-off. McKibben locals told me Times Square was hell on earth and convinced me not to go (still a bit pissed about that to be honest). Fahj had a party at his place, and I wore a T-shirt from a school production of *Grease* and Mickey Mouse ears without a hint of irony. I drank Sparks, no eggnog, not a drop of house party piss. We all piled onto the roof for our own 'ball drop' which was two guys I've never seen before holding a mirror ball. It was bitterly cold, so I started the countdown three minutes early, it's amazing what you can do with a voice that carries. I stayed up for hours. At some point, I toasted myself with a Vitamin Water and hailed a cab to JFK.

Having taken a rather large bite out of The Big Apple, possibly more than I could chew, I smuggled my New Year's hangover back across the Atlantic. Back to the shit-caked glamour of London. Back to the spacious accommodation for people who hate their money. Back to my paused adulthood. I had a lot of fun, but I never did make it to Cobrasnake.

My Dad

I always find the childhood sections of a memoir a little boring, divining some deep and nuanced meaning from the peccadillos of primary school, glimpsing some prediction of the adult being forged. Fashion designers will tell you they were always drawing dresses, vets say animals, as if the scribbles of infancy aren't almost exclusively people and pets. Architects love to tell you about building things, like you've never heard of Lego. Singers tell you they were always singing, as if none of us knew any nursery rhymes. So, when reading, I skipped Michelle Obama's prepubescence. I fast forwarded to Louis Theroux in sixth from. I'd prefer seven Harry Potter books that commence after Hogwarts if I'm completely honest.

It's also odd that we separate childhood and adulthood, as if at some point you mature and transition, shedding your child-skin like a snake and emerging as a different person. Maturity isn't a blank slate. Puberty isn't a memory wipe. Sudden cress-like tufts of hair on your goolies don't cause amnesia. I'm currently at the age where all my tufts are threatening to join together, but I'm still that same person I was as a kid. Everything that's happened has happened to one person. I find the separation odd.

Childhood is a considerable continent on the map of the self, and despite my glibness, you can't deny its sheer landmass. I think that's to do with having zero agency as a kid. You're just a person that things happen to, at the mercy of your guardians, you have no control. The lack of responsibility is delicious, it can be a trip, you can draw people and pets till the cows come home, but you're so vulnerable that you're defenceless against negative things too. It's really easy to fuck up rearing kids because they're soft little fuckers, sponges for discord, tablecloths that stain with your spills. I say this, but my childhood was fine. Nothing to really grumble about, nor any significant moments that foretold the man I am today, not in an overt way. My tablecloth is fairly spill-free. I was, for a time, obsessed with being a girl called Cathy. She was inspired by a Clearasil advert I saw, and had tonged ginger hair like when the cowardly lion gets ringlets. She, and by that I mean me, wore bridesmaids dresses and sang a lot, which I'd be obliged to talk about in NME interviews if I ever get signed. There are numerous pictures of me in dresses that I will never share.

As a man who loves men, my relationship with my dad is unsurprisingly complex. And not exactly current. I have reached a stage where we're in irregular contact (his birthday is on Christmas Day, so there's only a need for one obligatory annual check-in text) but he's not present in my daily life, nor considered in my big decisions, not whom I credit for where I've got so far. I've felt weird approaching this chapter because of the obvious significance of my father, this slightly estranged man who was so much more prevalent in my childhood, so key to my feelings, so instructive to my actions. I'm thinking through the years of compacted on/off influence, with fallow stretches of time without his scrutiny. And, like you, a whole chunk of my psyche is devoted to my parents, either in agreement or opposition. It's just that where my mum, who I lived with, was a rolling storyline like a soap opera, my visits to my dad are remembered in more distinct chapters. As a child of a breakup, you do compare parents, but my mum wins hands down. It's just that my dad, as a sideline player, could do star turns every other weekend. Rather than keep me fed and sheltered (no small task), he could make a fuss and buy my attention and affection (it was relatively inexpensive, I'm talking about the only childhood currency that matters: sweets).

Where to start? Being a kid, kid? Being an adolescent grasping at my limited independence? Being an adult which is just a rolling not-a-kid-anymore-ness with bills to pay? Before I was born, my dad got stabbed at the ice rink, and I've never shaken the imaginary image of his blood pooling out onto the frozen ice. It sounds like a crap school play, but must have been hugely traumatic. I can see the ripples of that event in his life now, still pooling, still spreading. He pretty much never leaves Brixton, it's a safe place for him, I only remember ever seeing him de-Brixton-ed once. On one occasion, he told me never to walk the same route home on consecutive days, because then people could easily plan when to jump you. Not fully paranoid, this sense of attack, because he was actually stabbed, but it does feel a bit cannabis psychosis too. My dad bought me desert boots when I was nine, and as we took them for a walk through the local patch of dry grass Lambeth council were calling a park, he asked me 'what would you do if someone tried to fight you right now?'. I said 'tell them to go away', which he insisted might not work. He's very secretive, or maybe just never saw me as need-to-know. I thought me and my half-sister were the only offspring. We went to the corner shop and he introduced me as his son and when the guy behind the counter asked how many kids he had, he said four. 'Four!?', I said as we left the shop. He said a woman had once claimed he was the father of her kid, a boy, but they lived far away. Sure Dad, but like wow, but like okay, but like-fine. Then we went back to his flat and he showed me a black and white photograph of two twin girls he'd fathered, it looked fucking old, like fifties old. And all I could say was 'Dad, if that woman had a baby and then there's these twins, and then there's me and my half-sister … that's five kids'. And he just giggled. And we never got to the bottom of it. Quartet or quintet? As I said, I was not need-to-know. And I have this odd ebbing, creeping feeling there's more. That I'll be at his wake and recognise my own features, that there'll be four or five or more people who clearly share my DNA, and we'll all be together again like re-joined slices of a Victoria sponge.

He took up martial arts. And steroids. I remember him really bulking up, which I'm sure isn't unconnected to being physically attacked, and becoming if not physically unapproachable, then at least the kind of guy you'd think twice about attacking. It's impossible to state quite how largely B. A. Baracus and Bruce Lee loomed in my childhood, those icons of male non-vulnerability. My earliest conscious memories of my dad are in full bodybuilder phase, eating smoothies of baby food and the bruises from bananas and egg whites. He fed the yolks to his cat Tibbs (we cannot deny my dad has a way with names). His house was stressfully lit with red, gold and green lightbulbs (very on-brand, but you were permanently struggling to see anything after 6 pm). His hallway was papered in a silver foil Egyptian Nile tableau, but the shiny surface did little to reflect the light. He had a fridge that was like a 1950s icebox, I remember it vividly, and still desire one of my own. And he was huge. Massive. All straining muscle and the Speedos you wear to compete (competition here is men flexing muscles at each other until one of them wins). I have loads of pictures of him competing, a numbered rosette clipped to his G-string, often in the pose you do right after you hit a golf ball, but his arms and legs are huge Coca-Cola Christmas hams. The observant of you out there might trace a line between this charade of hyper-masculinity and my own emerging homosexuality, but it had the opposite effect. I think part of the reason I don't like too much muscle, on myself or others, is because it reminds me of my dad. I don't hate built men,

I'm not allergic to the hench, they just remind me of my father in his Speedos doing a golf mime. And with the training and diet and body control and steroids and competition came the violence. Towards my mum. Nothing I ever saw, or remember, but categorically the reason we left London. And muscle to me has always felt slightly sinister, slightly menacing, slightly – potentially – violent.

When teenagerdom hit, my dad dropped the sweets act and brought me my first pager, which is unarguably cool, nothing I've bought before or since can come close to this translucent plastic symbol of status. I received maybe ten pages in the two years I had it, but that's beside the point. And for a brief period, our interests were aligned. He gave me my *The Miseducation of Lauryn Hill* CD and I remember being genuinely surprised it wasn't a fake from Brixton market. And visiting him from Brighton felt cool. Getting the train screamed independent woman (Pt. II). It was like I was a Londoner returning to my roots dem. But I didn't come up to town in my charity shop tat: my skinny jeans, tuxedo jacket and the white flat cap that I wore without a hint of irony. This was a specific epoch in fashion where people wore tennis wrist supports and golf visors to non-fancy dress parties. Visiting my dad, I would always lean into the sartorial masc. I adopted chav garments and ironic townie jewellery, reading *Heat* on the train, and binning it at Victoria station, ready to moonlight as a straight for a spell. My rendition of straight was patchy, several bum notes, but enough to pass for a few hours with my dad. I would not have ventured to Brixton in a dangly earring, that would have been a dead giveaway. Before the Great Wokeness I was considered camp – by classmates and teachers and the general populous – purely because I didn't conform to the limited scope of being a man. I was extroverted and expressive, rather than the steely blueprint of men controlling their emotions. I was never brooding, and that read as unmasculine. So I agreed with the consensus, I thought I was camp, but I was actually neither super camp nor super masc, I was something in the middle. These days we're (sort of) post these crushing gender stereotypes, and people don't care so much if you're not aggressively masculine. At least the people I know. I see Alan Carr on the telly, who I love, but I also think, no, I'm not this, I'm something else.

When I eventually moved back to London and, like any aspiring cool person, got heavily into vinyl, my dad gave me the pick of his records. Most of London was dressing like someone Pete Doherty would fuck, until that person became Kate Moss and nobody else stood a chance. I was dressing like a male Ronette, the destination being Little Richard at a party with Amy Winehouse, and I needed tunes to match. My dad gave me loads of Motown and Stevie Wonder. My mum's original Bowie records were shuffled into the stack, which seemed incredibly eerie, a sudden vision of my parents still in love, listening to Marvin Gaye and getting it on. Yuck. I reclaimed them for her just the same.

My dad's whole thing is hanging out, not really doing anything specific. Just cotching at his yard as the day passes. I can slip easily into the nothingness of the time with him, the TV and radio and glances at the paper. I cannot tell you a single thing that's changed in his life since I was six, which, as a paid up member of Generation Thrive's growth mind-set, is horrifying and comforting at once. Part of me still loves a cotch, but the time it takes to live the dream is all-consuming, there's only so much room for kicking back. Because of my dad's laid-backness, I always feel his untapped potential when I'm with him, a failure to fully launch, to strive for his aspirations. It's a reversal of the parent–child dynamic: the kid wanting to see the adult soar.

Is it awful to say that I don't particularly care if he's proud of me? It sounds like there's hidden malice or regret or anger yet to be managed, something meaty for my therapist and I to sink our teeth into. I've stopped needing and wanting his attention or approval, and I'm not sure how that came about, how I flipped from having a dad I idolised to having one more bedded in reality that fantasy. He is a good enough chap who happens to be my dad. I don't remember him being my hero, but surely, as my dad, he was? That's a default setting, I assume. It's impossible to be a man without looking towards your father, panning for clues to how it all works. My parents split up and there were two Ravens, a product of their disentanglement. The exuberant, excitable, loud, thoughtful Raven, and the one at my dad's house who was … smaller? The currency of exuberant, excitable and loud was badly spent with my dad, I had lower stock because his measure of my goodness felt adult and unattainable. I wonder if I partially detached before I can even properly remember? I wonder if it was a masculine energy that I already knew deep in my guts wasn't quite my agenda? I was thinking 'let's put on a play where I play all the characters and take on all the big numbers', he was thinking 'I'm making a man here'. I don't remember him having anything kid-friendly in his flat. I never drew dresses or pets because there was no colouring-in paraphernalia, no Lego, no holy dressing-up box for Cathy, just an adult life with adult stuff and a visiting kid who assimilated to that. I'm no psychologist but most kids of divorce (my parents never actually married) have dual identities. Most mixed raced kids do it too. And homosexuals. And anyone questioning the fabric of their gender. And women. And men. I'm not alone in the personality split, of dialling up or down my character thermostat depending on the climate. It's just glaring how extreme it was with my father.

Perhaps it's natural that I got less blinkered to my pre-set hero, and less adoring as I got older. Maybe I instinctively knew I wasn't going to get the return I needed. This was a man I saw a handful of times a year and I could bandage myself for those short periods. My dad, by way of circumstance and geography, couldn't apply the constant pressure you need to stop a wound bleeding out. I bled out with my mum, I was my fully saturated self, geysers of gayness spurting out of me (that sounds ruder than I thought it would).

And not just gayness, but I was granted all the me-ness possible, the choices of how to be, to flourish. A Dulux colour wheel of options. My time with my dad was more one-note, and he was so far away that it didn't feel like a pressing issue, a close threat. It was easier to just gradually give him less of my real self, and more of the version that appealed to him, which is either a cop out or a survival instinct or both. It pains me to admit that this summation, this ongoing question, is precisely the kind of conversation I usually have with a near-stranger at the end of a boozy dinner. 'My dad never loved me in the way I needed to be loved', I'll say to the half-friend before the concerned host discreetly calls me an Uber.

Obviously, I have unfinished business with my dad, but isn't unfinished business the heart of any family? Issues that felt so pressing at the time, that you've let go of in order to function happily, for the sake of familial equilibrium. I'm a man of action, but there's nothing for me to *do* here. There's no remedy for this silent father-son discrepancy. It's a frayed relationship, sure, but nicely cauterised family members are incredibly hard to come by. There's always unfinished business with a parent, or at least an ongoing amorphous relationship, a series of trials and errors and promises to yourself to be different next time. That's how life works. I can look back on this relationship with my dad, lit by the harsh LED of adulthood, rather than the Rasta lightbulbs. And though I feel something lacking, some missed potential, I'm not disappointed. I know what you're thinking, oh great another gay boy with unresolved daddy issues. But it does feel resolved to a point. The relationship is unpainful but not indifferent. Perhaps I zipped up my vulnerability, kept it from him, as a way to manage the cavities in my manliness he was trying to plug, a way of not even letting him see them. It's not been difficult because my father's presence has always been distant, in the rear-view mirror of my life, and it's only in the sitting and writing of this that it feels desperately close, larger than it appears.

The Kens

I know so many alright-looking gay men who seem sad under the muscle and it gets me down. They're all so tired of fighting their genetics, shell-shocked from going to war with their bodies. Veterans of the weights with a faraway look in their eyes, like they've seen too many squats. After all the gym straining, their veins pop and their physiques make a sad kind of sense. They're wider. They're leaner. Above all, they're peckier. Pecs are a delicious snack, flesh teacakes, chocolate button nipples. Breast bongos to bounce off. I want to say tiffin here, I'm not really sure what it is but it feels torso-y. These men toil for their tiffin tits. It's the by-product of doomscrolling, where they're fed squares of flesh that make them feel inadequate (I feel inadequate when I read Nora Ephron). But the feed creates a creeping sensation that you could be doing more, seeing more of the world with the plucky sidekick of great pecs. Pecs are currency, traded for attention. They give the impression of a naturally occurring, man-in-nature-who-lifts-things-in-order-to-live physicality. He fells trees. He jacks lumber. He can start a fire with nothing but a spool of cotton and a penknife.

My husband and I have some acquaintances we call The Kens. I say acquaintances because we haven't quite tipped into friendship, and we maybe never will if they find out about their nickname. You have to be incredibly careful with nicknames, in the same way you should screengrab Instagram posts and bitch about people over on WhatsApp, rather than accidentally reply to the original poster (I learned this the hard way, telling the lovely PR at a hotel that the room was weird because it didn't have a bin, which *is* weird frankly). The Kens are traditionally, undebatably, homosexually hot: big arms and big legs and they wear Speedos at the beach like it's no big thing. We met them recently in Greece, swimming off our private dock and trespassing into a luxury villa across the bay. As we climbed the cliff steps I had a chance to take in their Schwarzenegger bodies silhouetted against the sun. I posted a picture of them from a less porno angle and my DMs lit up like Guy Fawkes night (muscle is catnip for gays). They were hot. They *are* hot. They are The Kens. Everyone woofing in my DMs agreed.

In real life their bodies are overwhelming. The Kens have notable pecs, between the two of them there's four mounds of taut flesh, of man-udder salting in the sun. I glance at them when they're not looking. I shouldn't be looking but it's difficult not to. They're incredibly thoughtful, interesting, creative men, but their bodies feel almost constantly aroused, pulsing with red hot blood. That's obviously not to say you can't be intellectual and hot. But they're gentle men, quite tender and not at all shouty, while their bodies are screaming sex, bellowing arousal. They look like hench porn stars, hard all over like full-body erections. Boner bodies. It's both cartoonishly sexual, like Jessica Rabbit, and actually sexual, like sex. Fantastical, fabled, but right here in front of me. I don't want to have sex with them, but they are pure eroticism, they are human-sized pheromones, testosterone HRT. I know that to critique other people's bodies is not a great look, that one always sounds a little jealous commenting on the construction of someone else's hotness, that one is somehow sailing against one of the many waves of feminism on the good ship dysmorphia. But I'm not jealous, I'm captivated. I was somehow, somewhere built to fancy men, my sexuality smelted and forged in a certain mould, my arousal set in a certain shape. We can debate nature or nurture, my relationships with my mother and father, and the great, delectable spectrum that is human sexuality, but I fancy men, or the things that I understand to make men men, that's my thing. These men, The Kens, are men at their most manly, most physically unfeminine if we're looking at the binary base code of gender. And as a gay sponge, it's impossible not to soak it in. I wonder if they realise their Pamela Anderson effect? Of looking like the bodies you draw at school before your motor functions cement? Their hyper-sexualisation has to be deliberate. You can't spend that much time in the gym, in front of a mirrored wall, and not notice your body type is OnlyFans. They don't seem sad and overcooked, they are relaxed but rigid, and their bodies are a clear sign of the work they've done.

Pecs take time, and with all the things I like to do – writing about pecs, for example – time is a sparse commodity. Who has the hours in the day for pressing benches and the fake staircase at the gym? (I know the staircase isn't for pecs, but you have to balance your top body lest you become a Dairylea triangle.) I envisage my own journey to pecs, stages up the pec pyramid. I assume there'd be a dietary requirement for maximum pec-age, all chicken and spinach, six dozen eggs so I'm roughly the size of a barge, but I have a longstanding weakness for at-home high teas – wedges of rainbow coloured birthday cake with crunchy fondant and smooth buttercream arriving via Deliveroo. Drawn to the bright lights of the candles, legitimate birthdays got me hooked, and now, rather than a yearly treat, I think of birthday cake much like breathing, a regular necessity to keep me alive. God blessed me with the palette of a sugarholic nine-year-old, and I see no reason to pivot to health foods in order to Ken myself. Chicken breast in the pursuit of man breast? No thank you.

I'm never completely certain where I chart on the hotness scale, but pecs wouldn't do me any harm, let's throw perfume on the violet for the hell of it. The growing pains of my youth didn't yield pectoral muscles. God stretched me to six foot four and all I've got to show for it is zebra-ed marks on my hips and lower back. I'm sure I wanted a treasured chest in my teens. My fried eggs poached. My soft peaks set firm like meringue. I remember asking my dad for a string vest when I was eighteen (very Gwen Stefani 'Hollaback Girl') and him saying 'you actually need a little muscle for a string vest, Raven'. I was not a muscle teen. I was a weed in my dad's eyes, but then again he's never worked in fashion. Nowadays, like a Hollywood actress at the start of an interview, I would like to look good in a simple tee and not a scrap of makeup, without the help of Spanx or a Wonderbra. I don't need the actress's beauty secrets, the paleo regime, the personal training, the lunchtime facelift, I don't even need pecs, I just need my big break. Some Hollywood director to snap me up and cast me in a scene to steal with my palpable emotional rawness. There will be Oscar whispers but I won't make a thing of it. In the press junket for the film my scrap-less makeup will be noted.

I think of hot men the world over. The Pitts and the DiCaprios. The Hollywood Chrises and the Clooneys. The thirsty DMs I get about how hot my husband is would make you blush. And yes, obviously, he's attractive, but we're all biased towards vaguely muscular white men, towards a reflective blondness, towards the tell-tale signs of looking after yourself (pecs play a part, as do abs and cum gutters). And however regrettably I feel about it, I think about white men a lot. The way we (and I mean society at large) see them as hot by default, as the blueprint of hotness we're all riffing off. The way we think of fancying white men slightly outside the brackets of tall and young as a naughty indulgence. Pitt is fifty-two, for example; Rishi Sunak is non-white (naughty, naughty!); Tucci has no hair (get your freak on, girl!). But they all firmly live in the 'still would' camp. As a group they have a monopoly on society, and we all in some way protect that. We all find ourselves caught up in the general outrage that happens specifically when they're threatened or wronged. You see it all the time on TV career trajectory: an amazing ensemble cast wows us with their work but it's the white guy that gets the GQ cover, it's the white guy that gets the call from Hollywood. With *Girls*, for example, a show specifically focused on the emotional lives of millennial women, it's Adam Driver who's Darth Vader, the star warrior. This is a biased system, I bemoan its flaws, and yet all my boyfriends have been white men (not begrudgingly!). I find it so deeply irritating that my own system of desire hasn't moved me beyond the pale. I fancy Michelangelo's David, too. It's his solid torso, the marbled veins of his arms, the perfect chicken fillets. His huge hands are nothing to be sniffed at. He does have nice hair, doesn't he, the kind you'd run your fingers through if it weren't made of compacted granite. He certainly doesn't seem sad under the muscle like the other hots. Is it wrong to want to get felt up by a sculpture but not The Kens? Save me from myself.

Schoolboys

There are two types of people in the world: those who had a good time at secondary school, and those of us who like to be honest. It's not that I had a universally bad time from Year 7 to Year 11 – within that half-decade I'm sure there were good pockets, not just the can't-catch-my-breath belly laughter that comes immediately after getting stoned. While I try to remember some properly good things, here's a few impartial recollections. The standard uniform was cut from a vicious viscose with an overbearing thread count to keep us docile, but there was a (still inexplicable) trend for girls to layer up with very long knitted cardigans like bathrobes. The only markers of individuality were your bag and your shoes so we were all suitably obsessed with both. JanSport went unquestioned. Kickers were god tier. Nothing else mattered. (I lost a few friends when I brought my PE kit to school in a Sainsbury's bag.) The canteen served what can best be described as orphanage food, but I remember eating restorative custard creams by the double dozen on the way home. I wasn't a proper boffin, not a smarty-pants, nor was I bottom set, I once got an A– in Geography, but in retrospect I think the teacher thought I was someone else. Off-curriculum, I once had a Glyndebourne solo playing horny bedtime literature in ancient China (quite the casting). Most weekends I could be found playing some 007 platform game with gun-shaped controllers that I was frankly terrible at.

On the whole, school was a clusterfuck of adolescence, the hallways a gauntlet like the rapids in that Meryl Streep movie, a frothing soup of teenage venom and testosterone. Meanness was currency so people were unbelievably mean, meaner than *Mean Girls*. I say mean, but one of the biggest cusses of my school was calling someone a 'stig', which by modern parlance means grubby, or calling someone 'skanky', which meant the same. We were all saying the word 'gimp' at any available moment. I revisit these limp, not-that-mean insults here so that all former pupils can see how truly pathetic we were. In terms of meanness, I would at this point in time, like to offer an incredibly heartfelt *fuck you* to all the members of the 'I Hate Raven Club', you skanky gimps. I try not to wish badness on anyone, as I've promised myself to try and bring degrees of love and light into the world, but may all the 'I Hate Raven Club' members past and present have unsealing anal fissures and the kind of bad breath people talk about behind your back and never to your face.

With its intolerable peer-to-peer cruelty, school is of course a crash course in character-building, as sweet as it is sour. Everyone gets bullied because kids are always checking each other for weaknesses like Jurassic Park fences, a sort of pre-bullying like dogs sniffing each other's holes. Schooldays are spent trying to be brilliant whilst also signalling that trying to be brilliant is for idiots. And other kids just watch you, waiting for a chink in your weak teenage armour, for you to flash your Achilles heel like a Victorian woman. Nearly anything that marks you out as different is fair game to the legions of other pupils trying to both fit in and stand out. The success of your assimilation is constantly assessed, like a five-year job interview where the role is fitting in, a video game you complete when you stand out just the right amount. How loud you are. How quiet. How far you can push the uniform requirements. Whether you've been fingered.

I like to think that how you manage being pre-bullied (or how you survive it when bullies find purchase and you're fully piled upon), shapes your worldview for a long while. Perhaps you shrugged it off? Or dobbed them in? Or became a bully yourself? Or aligned with bullies so other bullies knew they couldn't touch you? Schools are prisons without the tattoos. Whose little bitch were you in order to survive? And how you coped at the time can somewhat dictate the way you manage conflict nowadays in the workplace or with your family. That default coping mechanism lasts right up until you have some proper therapy, either CBT or hypnotic regression. In the meantime, in the social hierarchy of secondary education, being snide was a superpower. As was being sporty. You already know the hellish warren of secondary school physical education. We'll get to that properly in a moment.

I once got accused of dealing drugs by a rather pious science teacher because she saw me 'passing something to someone else on the way to school' and honestly, looking back, this was a clear instance of racial profiling. The head of year, a man with a bushy moustache and a near-constantly incredulous face, called my mum in 'for a chat', which is never great. To give you a sense of time period, my mum *paged* me to tell me to come home immediately for an interrogation disguised as another 'chat', but I was busy traipsing the local precinct listening to Nirvana's *Nevermind* on a Discman (a CD I'd selected from a large book of translucent envelopes) and buying single cigarettes for 35p a piece. Anyway, I wasn't dealing drugs so much as being brown, which the poor science teacher had understandably conflated, bolstered by the circumstantial evidence of me having my hand near another pupil's. Nothing is as infuriating as being accused of something you didn't do, it's an exquisite pain, and I remember all instances of unfiltered, impotent rage from being wrongly accused. The time a boy told the caretaker I had called said caretaker a faggot still gnaws at me with the ferocity of a thousand rats. The caretaker took punishment into his own hands like some sort of maintenance worker vigilante. Sadly for me, this was his *Joker* moment. He made me stand in the corner for the whole of lunchtime, whispering in my ear that he knew where I lived, which was absolutely terrifying, a cruel strategy unsanctioned by Ofsted. Perhaps this is an understandable reaction for a man worn down to the nub by years of sweeping up glitter, chipping at hardened UVA glue and the emasculation of the overflowing infant toilets. This is why when I'm finally in prison I hope it's for a real crime like a bank heist or romancing the inheritance out from under a family of note à la Anna Nicole Smith. Speaking of incarceration, I've never been violent, but I have this constant paranoia that the day I finally cave in and punch someone, I will accidentally kill them because such is my luck. It will either be the explosive power of all the historical non-punches built up like sedimentary rock in my fist – basically a thousand punches in one – or the person will just fall weirdly, perhaps into the path of a steamroller. A life sentence for murder is fair, it doesn't really matter whether you've punched before or will punch again. I will take my prison medicine if that happens, living off gruel in solitary until I find God and numerous horny pen pals to bigamise. In fact, most of my secondary education centred around avoiding violence, of dodging punches like Mike Tyson, so thank you to my most thuggish classmates (the ones with the Reebok Classics), in a roundabout way you've saved a man's life.

A miscarriage of justice at a secondary comprehensive is less life-shattering, and I think most of the science faculty were out to get me (they never let me be the first person on the Van de Graaff generator, but that might just be a fine hair thing). I had two types of teacher at school: those who thought I needed raising up like Simba on Pride Rock, and those who thought I needed bringing down a peg or two. Secondary school was easier because I only had to endure hour-long lessons with the 'bring him down a peg' faction. My primary education, on the other hand, was marred by year-long teacher feuds, escapable only by summer holiday and a week in the Lakes (it rained the whole time and our tent collapsed and we had to sleep in the car but it was still better than a school day with Mrs Redacted). And maybe I wasn't what you'd call a star student? I remember applying to be Head Boy, but having so few honourable mentions under my belt, I just suggested they should probably have a Black student in the head pupils (it didn't work, which is for the best, and the slots were filled by Sports and Blondes). Maybe I should hold my hands up, maybe I should empathise with their fight to educate me? Can I look back at my secondary education with the knowing eye of an adult? I appreciate it's annoying, as an appointed educator, to have a very disruptive and gobby boy in your class whose grades are solid Bs. He's complacent, sure, but, like most men, he'll flourish if you praise him. I know you're tired, dear teacher, but if you can see beyond the gob, if you challenge him and intrigue him, he will excel, he might even be a token of Black excellence for your majority-white school. This didn't happen. I remember the French teacher who did a monologue about the bad apples – *pommes horribles*, if you will – ruining the learning experience for the entire batch of students, while shooting daggers at me (and only me) across the room. A girl behind me caught the evil stare in her eye like Harold at Hastings and the teacher had to clarify that she was 'talking about Raven Smith, aren't I Raven Smith?'. For the record, it's impossible to play devil's advocate when someone's using your full name and staring at you. But I maintained my B in French.

It was on the sports field where things really went to shit. Friday was PE day, straight after Art, which I loved for its rigorous curriculum of copying Cubism. But this angular joy was overshadowed by the incoming storm of an hour outside with only the boys out on the pitch. I remember feigning illness every Friday morning, such was the curse of the sports field – a cough, a headache, ambient nausea, I once tried to break my leg with a chest of drawers for six weeks PE-free (my efforts yielded a light bruise). I have hated many things in my short years on this planet, but none have come close to the abhorrent ritual of putting a peerage of pubescent boys on a field to compete every week.

This was at a time before I had the clear understanding that I was a gay, mainly because I was so horny that everything turned me on. I remember the first time I orgasmed, and the newfound adulation I had for my body and its new mechanism for transcendental, if not incredibly brief, *petite morts*. I remember looking at all the other boys, my peers, wondering if they had cum yet, if they were in the cum club. Which of us were officially men? Which of us still boys? Who had made the wet dreams of Sex Ed into wet realities? I have no idea if this is a normal way to experience the world once you've single-handedly brought yourself off, but I'm glad it's no longer a secret that occupies space only in my head. I wasn't officially gay, but I knew I wasn't like the other boys, and not in an exciting superhero way.

And at secondary school puberty crescendos. You either get tits or your balls drop. I appreciate there's a whole spectrum of gender, in the same way art isn't just Cubism, but at school you're dumb and you just pick one of these camps and hope to transition into adulthood as unnoticeably as possible with your deep voice or huge rack. Society sort of expects us to fall into easily recognisable stereotypes early on – the jock, the hot girl, the goth and the others from the Breakfast Club. Nearly every teen drama reinforces this. You are Buffy or AC Slater. And as you ripen, you dress differently. There's the grand tradition of the post-pubescent girl: dressing like a slut to see how it feels. If the hemline is nearer the epicentre of pheromones, will more people notice her? How much leg is too much? For men it's different. Men want to dress so that they look as similar to other men as possible, with as little differential deviation from traditional manliness. To stand out is to fail, so it's literally unfitted trousers and unfitted shirts in infinite circulation. Adidas poppers at a stretch. I guess it's tribal to dress like each other, but you need an anthropologist for that take to have any real weight. I was just a boy who wanted to fit in, hence the bulky shirts. Can we all agree that in Year 9, we were all trying to work out how our bodies worked in context to the rest of the world? That was the main objective, alongside our mocks.

Outside the deeper voice, traits of physical manliness start to emerge, but you can only see them just before PE when you all have to take off your clothes. Honourable mention here to the PE teacher (male, great thighs) who said, 'last one in the shower's a woofter'. I wasn't the last one in the shower, lest my wayward sexuality be unveiled, but this was still very triggering. Changing before PE is the moment the protection of your starchy school uniform falls away and you're left with a near-hairless mortal coil. Male bodies are on display, ready to contrast and compare. Are your nipples normal? Does everyone have back spots? What the fuck is that muscle mass? How did he get abs? Some of you are still kneading the dough of boyhood, others are proved loaves of adolescence, none of you have the stale moobs of middle age.

You'd think if I could dig deep enough into my loin memory, perhaps through Derren Brown hypnosis, I'd be able to remember some pang of desire or titilation, some visceral reaction to the bodies and testosterone, the full bottoms on display. But I only remember fear. Absolute fear. Of the body I suddenly inhabited, and its museum quality display just before PE. Sometimes on a rainy afternoon in Superdrug, I'll catch a whiff of Lynx Africa and be transported back to the hideous naked carousel of my youth. On the cusp of adulthood, your junior body becomes

a foreign land, the plains are shifting and there's new vege-
tation and you're discovering all of it like Columbus. But at
precisely the same time your living corpse becomes an alien
landscape, abducted by new hormones, you're forced to
show it to other people in the showers. What should be a
transformative thirty-second puberty montage in a film,
becomes a lived reality. It's one thing to be a naked adult,
with all the sticky vulnerability that comes with that, but a
new teenage body is like an Internet impulse-buy that
doesn't quite fit and you're trying to style it out. It's not that
you've all become adults, not by a long shot, you just have
grown-up paraphernalia where your extremities meet your
torso.

Physical maturity isn't the same as sexual experience.
Everyone in a secondary school is a dormant sex doll, a
tessellation of erogenous zones, a one-man-band who can't
find the tune (despite lots of fiddling). We were sexless teenagers, because teenagers don't have sex, at least not real sex.
If, by some divine intervention, other people engage with
you sexually, you still haven't completed all the levels, you're
still beta testing. You do the sex act, the penis in orifice
thing, but it's not really about enjoyment, or taking your
time, it's more about the exact mechanic. I fully recognise
that the only two lesbians at my school coupled up and
eschewed penis completely. They used to snog right by the
school gates and it was the talk of the quad for a week,
which is a decade in the dog-years of school life. I don't
know enough about woman to woman sex to tell you if

they too are beta testing at fourteen, but I assume we were all novices applying for apprenticeships. All of the delicious exploration of sex is years away (and behind closed doors). In the showers, you measure the slow development of physical masculinity in sprouting armpit hairs, the sexualised-selves of your classmates emerging. But alongside that testosterone-driven physicality something else was incubating: competition. It's impossible, at this stage in my development, to differentiate between the horrors of the naked male body, and the horrific naked ambition of all men.

Men can't be men without establishing some hierarchy of physical manliness, like lions in a pride. To define this pecking order, boys of secondary school age are pitted against each other on the playing field. It's like gladiators without the spears or breastplates or eventual ascension to Valhalla. Team-picking is notoriously harrowing (see the entire Woody Allen filmography for specific ramifications), because there's a pack mentality of explicitly ranking the herd and assigning the top dogs. The most physically superior guys have the job of categorising the group: from the most strong, powerful and exacting, to the weakest and least coordinated. The competition is rampant, based on an intricate configuration of general sporty prowess and past performances on the pitch. I'm not sure of the curriculum vitae of each team captain who wielded their selectional powers, but the freakish pastime of participating in sports *outside of school* was a common denominator. Their job was to create opposing teams cream-first, separating the curds and whey of masculinity. The mice. The men. Other outside-of-school exercisers, some of which entered into fabled non-school 'championships', were picked first. The rest of us were creamless semi-skimmed milk, split into boys who exercised on purpose and the friends of anyone who'd already been picked. There was always a scrabble, a race to the bottom, a desperation not to pick the worst boy (you know the type, I'm afraid). There is such a badge of dishonour for getting picked last for PE, but I would say the rising anxiety of last-pickage touched most of the bottom third. We all have our scars.

Unsurprisingly, I learned almost nothing from my prescribed physical education. Six boys circuiting a snowy field jointly carrying a bench never felt like a learning experience or a moment of growth. Cross-country was dreadful, too, my teacher driving to the furthest-away part of the course to do a second register as we wheezed past. Two words guaranteed to strike fear into the heart of anyone I know are 'bleep' and 'test'. I once made a girl faint by punting a ball she was bending to pick up and kneeing her in the head. I'm searching for a positive experience, and all I've got is that I didn't actually die all the times I thought I would – hypothermia, heart attack, not approaching a javelin from the side.

There's a long established male obsession with sport and the desire to win. To run faster, lift heavier, kick more accurately. School sport is just a microcosm of professional sport. If men do it well they get cups, or a black belt, or get to be 'top of the league', which matters hugely. It's phallic, of course. Bats and rackets are an extension of the penis, the balls are the balls. Football is kicking, which maybe has something to do with cavepeople killing animals. Boxing is literally men punching each other (in high-waisted cute shorts). Blood is welcomed. Crying is tolerated. Men create gods out of the other men who are better at kicking or lifting or putting. Strength and stamina. Accuracy and precision. It's all fertilised with power and dominance. Sport is actually just about mathematics, the angles of snooker, the trajectory of a tennis ball. But sports zealots don't want to admit trigonometry. They want the hand of God. They want golden balls.

Sportsmen will talk about teamwork, of clubbing together like vets in the trenches, but the physically less-than aren't part of that camaraderie. They're left on the side-lines, with knitted scarves and vuvuzelas to showcase their admiration. You can be terrible at sports and still exceed at competitiveness, screaming at a hockey stick or a 'blind' referee. In my early twenties, I avoided going to the pub when the football was on for fear of second-hand male aggression, non-footballers still antagonised by a ball and a net, clinging to their fourth pint and a long-lost life on the pitch. At kick-off, the valve of pent-up aggression is opened and bled like a radiator, spitting out across the pub floor and occasionally the streets too. Everyone at the pub has nine-to-fives but a livestreamed match on Sky Sports turns them into Cantona ready to scissor-kick a spectator (the scissor-kicked man was an alleged racist, and I have conflicting feelings about scissor-kicking racists. Can I still get into Valhalla if I punch a Nazi under a steamroller? Makes you think). I often think about the aggression and speed of male basketball versus the stagnant rules of netball forced on girls. Telling women 'do not move when you have the ball' reeks of patriarchy, no?

The weirdest thing about the grand tradition of school sports, is that I wasn't physically bad at them. My peers were mini-men made of beef and muscle, but I was a palatable lean mince. I don't have a problem with back-of-the-net accuracy, or dexterous flexibility. Gymnastics, yes. Athletics, sure. I can basket a ball because I'm tall and closer to the net, but I am categorically not available for masculine competition. You simply cannot deny that vuvuzelas are fun, only an outright fun sponge could resist their mythological siren call, but I don't allow the bandwidth for the macro-competitiveness of straight men. I don't have a competitive bone in my body, unless you count that one Smirnoff Iced night with this guy from Eggham, but that's another story. My athleticism, on the whole, is selfish, verging on narcissistic. It's all for me. I love to run, not race. I like exertion, not events. Training, not track meets. Okay, there was a time before puberty when running past people on sports day was a thrill (I actually waved en route to the finish line). But it's not about winning for me. Nor is it about taking part. I'm never happier than when I'm sprinting for pleasure, not because I'm late. I just like the feeling of running free like a dumb Labrador with the whiff of pedigree chum on the wind, running free like the Challenger space shuttle taking off, running free like the liquid terminator in *Terminator 2*. Bugs splatting into my eyeballs as I gallop forwards. I love the exertion, the spike in endorphins, the heaving chest of the recovery. What I don't love is someone else next to me, someone else to consider. Wait, is running very fast the same as my teenage sex life? I can't stop thinking of myself. It doesn't matter as long as I reach the finish line.

As a Black kid, aka a Black man in the making, there was an expectation at school that I'd be sporty. Aggressively sporty. Stress on the aggressive. If you're a Black, tall teenager with limited distribution of fatty deposits, people don't see a man, they see a sportsman, a winner. Okay, sometimes they see a drug dealer, but on the whole they see an athlete, an unbridled powerhouse that just needs channelling. There was a surge from teachers and students alike to force me to conform to the stereotype of assertive and agile Black men. I should invoice for the time I spent wheedling out of direct competition, or dodging the teachers that said 'you should try out for basketball'. Okay my school didn't have try-outs, we just had thirty normal-height white boys and me, which was initiation enough to the team. Men simply don't understand how you could be physically capable of sports, but not interested in dominating the field. It's just a disconnect for them, because they're conditioned to dominate physically, that's how they win. Obviously, I know loads of men that aren't striving to be top dog, to dwarf the rest of the herd, but at school with its limited options, being the strongest, or fastest, or most sporty was the goal. I have always opted out of this particular tributary of masculinity. I would always say good luck to everybody else at the start of sports day, which is apparently a sure sign of weakness (I still won).

I'm not sure if there's any real consequences to defying the male expectation to excel physically. We could reasonably ask what the point of being good at anything is if it's not tested in a measured way? It's like revising for your GCSEs and bunking off the exams. But I'm happy not to quantify my physical prowess. I'm happy jumping and not knowing how high, jogging without knowing how far. I don't want to sound naff, but by choosing deviation from competitive sport, and competitive manliness, I think I've won my own sort of medal (that does sound a bit naff). But I've won at refusing to compete, my own black belt in being myself. This has severed some masculine ties for sure. My dad simply cannot understand why I never sharpened my natural abilities and took them all the way to, I dunno, the Olympics? I am, I think, less of a traditional man for refusing the starter pistol, for running my own course. But absolutely best of luck, I guess, to those still competing.

Hungry

I'm at my mate's house in Berlin and we've immediately fallen into a synchronised co-habitation. I have indoctrinated him to my ways, while respecting the majority of his boundaries. We communicate almost exclusively via song lyric bellowed from the neighbouring room; we gift each other Cornflake Ritter Sport; I help him vet prospective lovers on apps; we spend an inordinate amount of time sharing screen-grabs of potentially game-changing leather trousers. I'm mainly eating pumpernickel bread with processed cheese slices, oval tomatoes cut into finger wedges, and curry flavoured hummus from the Kaufland supermarket. I tell my temporary flatmate I'm swapping the bread out for corn cakes, that all the wheat is slowing my thinking down, it's holding me back. 'My friend does that,' he says, 'she's anorexic'. 'No, no,' I say, 'it's the gluten. I'm being careful with gluten. It ferments inside you, like it keeps cooking or proving or whatever after you've eaten it, and you balloon'. He can hear the crazy. I can hear the crazy. I nudge back to the kitchen, embarrassed, to snack on some gluten-free health food biscuits with the flavour profile of sweet cardboard.

It'll come as no surprise to you that men and women don't eat the same, our diets are as gendered as a French dictionary. When we frequent restaurants, normally dolled-up on double dates, the genders split. Men, as you well know, need fuel for war: bloodied steaks and fists of fries. Nothing too fancy, three storeys maximum: bread, meat, bread (an obligatory slice of tomato to ward off scurvy). A man's diet needs a hint of violence for the nutrients to hit like a Roman gladiator or Braveheart. Cowboys can be found out back, tearing strips of raw meat, as smoke swirls from the primal fire of a barbecue (at a push, a McDonald's abattoir can do a lot of the messy gristle work).

While men are from Mars bar, women are from cleanness, eating things they've gathered rather than hunted. Women, the fairer sex, prefer to have salad, or legumes eaten raw, or foraged berries. Salad can be purchased pre-chopped to avoid the gradual bulk on an upper arm. For women, the garnish is the main course, pushing juliennes round a tiny plate, maybe the occasional petal, pretending not to care about the food. Men are so brave that they'll also eat this feminine salad if it's been barbecued, aggressively fired on the outside and charred to a manly carcinogenic crisp.

Of all human sustenance, seafood knows no gender. Something in the saltwater de-sexes everything and even the cockles lose their innuendo. Mussels and octopus and shrimp are neutral gods, carb-free for women but man-scavenged from rock pools. Oysters are vaginas, there's no two ways about it, but I guess prizing them open with a dagger-y shucker is masc. Men are blessed with having a constitution too strong and manly for food poisoning and can sink raw oysters till the cows come home. Men use this protein-y steak spike to stomp around making an impact, while women just get smaller and smaller like Borrowers. It's worth saying here that these are all solid facts, you don't need to Google them, just take my word for it.

Before wellness gave us a modern vocabulary for restriction and starvation, before keto and paleo and superfoods and macronutrients, people just wanted to be thin. I can't believe I'm saying this but for the longest time, looking like you were being ravaged by a heroin habit was seen as chic. You didn't ever just say you wanted to be thin out loud, that was always seen as gauche. The code word was 'being careful'. You were being careful in Pret. You were being careful at dinner. You 'forgot' to eat breakfast. I don't know for sure if people these days are more anxious or less anxious about muffin tops and gapless thighs. I watch films and red carpets and wonder if we've really outgrown our size zero ideals. Society is so steeped in thinness, so marinated in anti-fat, it's enough to put you off your master cleanse lemonade.

Before strong became the new thin, I worked in fashion-adjacent offices where everyone over twenty-five was on a fad diet. It was Atkins at a bare minimum and everybody smoked like a chimney while drinking a daytime Diet Coke or night-time vodka soda. People got very excited about alfalfa sprouts and scallions and the discovery of something flavourful or sweet with minimal calories (today's vaping is the natural evolution of this phenomenon). It was an office-wide culture of tiny portions. Miniscule. I'd say crumbs but crumbs are carbs. The diets weren't healthy, and neither was the office atmosphere, starved as it was of fuel. (The upside of this for any budding writer is that it's a piece of piss to pitch food stories at fashion mags because whoever gets your email is hungry.) Conversely, everyone *under* twenty-five was burning through hormones and shot gunning ham and cheese baguettes, barely chewing the bread. It felt like a tiny act of rebellion in a hungry office.

But it was definitely infectious, this hush-hush restrictive climate. Everyone can be a raging non-eater in a fashion, but you can never talk about it. Because of the cardinal sin of talking directly to a woman about her body, of open, unfurtive judgement, we all just did it behind each other's backs. We said 'nice jacket'. We complimented palazzo trousers. We retreated to our lairs (Blackberry messenger) and noted everything. The not-thinnest of us would point out other marginally thinner women to highlight their lack of control. 'She looks painfully thin', we'd say sadly, before forgetting to have lunch. We speculated that a very thin woman we all knew was fully anorexic, fully nil by mouth, but was having regular vitamin injections which explained her unbroken lustrous hair. The idea was to stay just the right side of the grimly fine line between tiny and dying.

As is tradition, everyone in an office gets a cake for their birthday (usually Colin the caterpillar), and full slices in napkins were often left near keyboards to be disappeared by the cleaner. One woman, without saying a word beforehand, got flowers for her birthday instead of cake. She looked hungry, but she didn't eat a single rose. That's real discipline. You'd think I'd be above these manic antics, but as a wannabe It-girl, I was torn between adequate nourishment and being one of those super-thin persons people worry about. I'm not sure it's possible to be both. When I started in the office, I'd hunch over jacket potatoes with beans and cheese and coleslaw, the holy trinity of spud toppings. After a year, I was living off soup and prawns and thanking Jesus I wasn't a woman because I associated that with menstrual cycles and the dreaded notion of emotional eating. Imagine being so hungry you're glad you don't have emotions, that you're not led by them to eat, that they're dulled. That food is fuel rather than a sensory delight. Anyone outside of fashion would see me being careful (refusing potatoes at dinner, eating only the interior of a sandwich) and look at me like I were mad, but I couldn't see the madness, I could only trust in my illusion of control.

As I approached thirty, I was paranoid that I had finally stopped growing, that all my beansprout vitality was used up, and that the energy I ingested just hung around in my body like the Gulf War Jarheads that never got to fight. I was convinced I'd reached an imaginary sell-by date, or use-by date, both my body and face on the turn. The month before I got married all I ate was sugar snap peas and occasional slices of Gouda when I got so hungry I wanted to bark. I became genuinely happy my face was a mass of angry angles, pure cheekbone. Why smile when you can pout? Rather than buy new jeans, I started ruching them with a belt. I was convinced that I was thin but I didn't *dress thin* because that was gaudy. I honestly felt like the denial of my desires was my power, that the restrictions made me stronger, that there was method within the disordered. I don't remember much external reinforcement of my newly bordered eating (one assumes this happened on Blackberry messenger), but at one point I was congratulated for ordering meatballs at a lunch, as if they're the naughtiest of treats. In fairness, I thought they were carb-free. I recently saw some former colleagues at the pub and they were genuinely surprised to see me drinking a pint, such was the militant forcefulness of my vodka soda years.

I know this all sounds a bit dark, a bit grim, but when you force down your biological need for nourishment, your body is so vigilant for snacks you get kind of high. The upside of semi-starvation is that you're so hungry you're nut-nut. Many religious ceremonies involve some type of fasting, and I saw God every time I said no to a starter, no to a pudding. Whatever you're up to – private messaging on your Blackberry, buying superior palazzo pants, throwing cake in the bin – your eyes are searching the periphery for berries to scavenge and squirrels to barbecue. The hunter-gatherer in your evolutionary biology cannot be silenced, nor frankly should it be. As you compulsively julienne, you're fighting the primal urge to live and prosper.

Consistently under-eating (something I couldn't manage long-term) is also coupled with an inability to approach anything in a rational way. I think of that time as aesthetically resplendent and emotionally fraught because I didn't have the energy to cope with anything. I had bundles of nervous energy, which is not the same as being energised. It's like saying you're nervous happy, or nervous peaceful, or nervous tired. You nervously leave the office to nervous-commute home to nervous-sleep. People tend not to be nervous relaxed as a rule. It's not nice to be hungry and not do anything about it, to avoid the one thing you need: a meal. It's the worst feeling. Every diet fad is basically people trying to lose weight without being hungry because hunger sucks, it's one of the most miserable states. The not-so-secret secret to weight loss is hunger, but we'd do anything to avoid that.

And hungry is where we find ourselves at least three times a day. Breakfast, lunch and dinner. The naffness of a brunch, the intricacies of a high tea. I'd love to say I have an elevated palate, and at times I do eat quite fancily, but generic classics still comfort me. Salmon and potatoes, roast dinners, six-minute eggs. Actually, eggs are not so much a problem, as an obsession. As with many of my stone tablet beliefs, I heard conjecture, took it as fact, and immediately adopted it into my daily routine. (This is one of the reasons I don't wear cork Birkenstocks, but love the plastic ones.) My current egg-wisdom originally came from an interview with Londoners about their personal trainers. When a PR guy from Hackney said 'the best multivitamin is an egg' my world shifted. Eggs, I nodded, yes, eggs. I still say the best multivitamin is an egg as if it's a pure fact, the eleventh commandment they didn't have the space to chisel. Despite crumby one night stands, job uncertainty, ongoing abandonment issues with my father, an egg has never let me down. I like poached eggs that remind me of the shaved nutsack of an Essex boy, gooey omelettes the texture of raw liver, and scrambles on craggy husks of sourdough. I get genuinely anxious when we're down to two eggs at home. Half a dozen in the box and I sleep easy. I could happily live off spicy veg and eggs if castaway on a desert island, I wouldn't need the best songs of my life or the bible, I'd just need chickens and a pan.

When you're an only child with a single-parent mother, there are very few occasions where she cooks something you don't like. You're not a fussy eater *per se*, you just have a conspiracy of two not to whip up unlikable foods. Weirdly the foods I used to hate as a kid are now the core of my diet – eggs, tomatoes, nuts, fish, the odd banana. I'm trying to work out what I did eat back then, and I think it's bacon pasta? And actually, I stopped eating bananas because a chap at work described their blood sugar spike as *finger pointing up* *finger pointing down* and I see his digits whenever I'm in the supermarket. Bananas, incidentally, are a great metaphor for relationships because they gradually get worse for you – sugarier and more GI spiking – as the days pass, the glucose slowly revealing itself. Hidden sugars are the pits. You know where you stand with the sugar in Haribo. I'd rather eat Starmix and ride the wave.

My transition from being a pedestrian fussy eater to a semi-foodie happened when I got a kitchen porter job. I loved being a pot wash, it was the moment I realised cooking could be so much more than 'add some pickled onion Monster Munch to that immediately'. It was the summer I was sixteen, the promising twilight between Year 11 and sixth form, a window where you legitimately had the chance to reinvent yourself (it was Madonna's Marlboro Man era, and we were all inspired). After accidentally outing me to the entire body of staff, a barwoman took a shine to me and would secret me gin and tonics in the dumb waiter like it was still prohibition. I would open the lift and pour them down the sink because they were disgusting. I have yet to meet a sixteen-year-old with a taste for gin and/or tonic. Like all new drinkers, I needed sugar to disguise alcohol's bitter truth. I was an Archers and cranberry teen, a double vodka coke at a push, never, ever a vodka soda. My day shifts were interspersed with drum'n'bass nights (was I Brighton's only drum'n'bass twink?) and sneaky dabs of MDMA, but I spent Saturday Kitchen mornings, morbidly hungover, lugging sacks of potatoes and pulling the anal beards out of mussels. The thing I remember most accurately are the mountains of vegetables that needed my attention. Readying myself to tackle an Etna of carrots, hand-peeling a supernova of garlic cloves, or chopping a forest of parsley. The remedial, repetitive tasks may have been therapeutic had my serotonin not been dramatically slumping, homeostasis curdling my mind. Saturday afternoons were centred on washing up. Miserably scraped plates would arrive by the crate-load ready to be jet-washed. Chefs would throw hot skillets at you like Olympic discuses. I found myself un-ironically polishing ten thousand spoons. I once remembered that we'd need to bake another batch of frozen baguettes mid-service and the head chef promoted me on the spot based on my incisive pluck. I was no longer a KP, I was a cold chef (I didn't do hots outside of microwaving puddings). Key life skills from that time include learning how to deep fry and realising you can stir tomato sauce directly into molten cheese and make a sort of pink cheese on chips. It took a while for my palate to mature like cheddar but I did develop a lifelong panache for salads. Do you ever cook something from scratch and realise how heart-attacking-ly bad it is for you? The kitchen taught me this, too. The smear campaign about how they make McDonald's has a nugget of truth to it. The butter in millionaire's shortbread would make your toes curl. And butter makes the world go round. Every chef-cooked meal on your plate is laced with butter because it's delicious. It's on the potatoes, it's under the fish, it's hiding in the sauce like a private detective, ready to glaze your arteries.

There's a romantic idea around professional cooking, it's a practical art, full of flair, bustling with imagination. All sips of sauce off spoons, delicate adjustments in flavour, smacking your lips and talking in a French accent. The rat from *Ratatouille*. Men who can cook are fit, right? Chef whites are sexy. There's a chef I know in Paris who would absolutely get it. It's not the cut of his figure, the shape of his dough, it's his commitment to food. There's this obsession with men who display small acts of creativity. Actually, all creatives are deities these days, gods among the uncreative mortals. It's to do with their dexterous hands, engaged minds and enduring attention. Creatives concentrate for great periods of time on very specific things – books, films, paintings, sharing plates. How is that not slightly sexual? It's a passionate life, that somehow translates to a passion for sex, for me. Who doesn't want to be noticed? Who doesn't want to be delicious?

Don't get me wrong, chefs are very hot and steamy and skilled. But something happens to jobbing chefs. They aren't here for the art, they don't give a fuck. Or maybe that's not quite true. Many of the chefs in my kitchen started out with artisanal hopes – sous chefs with big dreams, juliennes layered like fine brushstrokes, butter sculpted like a Rodin – but something about the grind of cheffing whittled the art down to a splinter, a post-meal toothpick. Few of the chefs I knew came through the repeated brutality of weekend services unscathed. I guess that's why they call it the cordon blues.

Despite the hygiene regulations, professional kitchens are some of the most toxic places on earth. There's a hierarchy borrowed directly from the army, where you just shit on the person below you (metaphorically if you want to keep your hygiene certificate). Kitchen life is not about magnanimity and listening, it's about shouting down. Think of the Sergeant Major-ness of Gordon Ramsay. Chefs are like this but have none of the luxurious trappings of fame. They lack the followers or reach. Their only audience is the other chefs and everybody is chronically angry, performing masculinity with the zeal of Kenneth Branagh discovering an unpublished Shakespeare play. I wonder if they were just a touch overheated? Regardless of the extraction fanning, because of the layers of aprons and those thick cotton chef's whites, your sweat is somehow channelled and runs down your back and into your boxers (everyone wore boxers in 1998). We all called this Wolf Arse, because it was so irritating it made you howl like a wolf. At 2 pm on a Saturday everyone had Wolf Arse, but the chefs I worked with howled for other reasons too. Every chef was self-diagnosed as misunderstood, an overlooked food prodigy, a roasted chicken with clipped wings. They were the one working the hardest. They were the one working the fastest. And they were all angry about getting constantly shat on, the trickle-down defecation, and exhausted from shitting on everyone else. Everyone but the head chef was frustrated that they weren't the head chef (our head chef smoked crack in the staff loos which lent a certain chaos to the hierarchy).

Chefs are primeval cavemen, supernaturally obsessed with having the sharpest knife, and the most aggressive burn scars on their hands are their war medals. They don't so much use a mallet to pulverise meat, but become the mallet, smashing through the kitchen with their overbearing personalities. There's a lot of brute force that scatterings of salt fail to cure. Cold chefs like me were chicken shit, because wielding the great fires of the range was the trophy. Microwaving puddings (quite efficiently, I might add) didn't cut the mustard.

I know there's wonderful kitchens out there, but most gastropubs have a cell of simmering men in synthetic white jackets sweating their tits off with Wolf Arses and ready to bite the teeth out of your mouth. It's the opposite of the flour and fauna of the Bake-Off tent with its perfectly-crumbed fruit scones and craft learning. Not to say that women aren't arseholes who shit all over a kitchen, but the energy is distinctly male. The bad kind that's just a constant exertion of power and dominance. The noxious culture of cheffery was my first foray into the way adult men act when there's no women around. All yin, no yang. The indiscretion of an exclusively testicular climate. We once heard on the radio about a corrupt gynaecologist who'd been arrested for groping a huge slew of his patients and one chef said 'Who could blame him?'. I pretended I hadn't heard and kept peeling. There was another chef who was rumoured to have a big dick because 'he's so fucking ugly, God must have balanced it out somewhere', which is less misogynistic but still. There's actually a lot of dick chat in a kitchen, it's clunkily Freudian, but nobody really mentions their own. There's no safe space to share truth, no 'am I normal?', it's much more about posturing. Ali G was massive at the time and one chef would signal to the hole in a doughnut and say 'this is your batty, batty-boy'. This was the 'humour' of the workplace, essentially comparing kitchen items to body parts. Pointing at a shrivelled saveloy and saying 'your dick's here, mate' was *chef's kiss*. Anything phallic was fair game and God had blessed us with an abundant harvest of dick-like veg – courgettes, cucumbers, carrots, aubergines, marrows, sweetcorn (parsnips at a push if you're desperate). We described scalding pans as 'hot as a witch's tit', which I still say because it's so wonderfully goddamned visceral.

Overall, the kitchen dynamic is jovial, you're all comrades in the culinary trench, but scratch the surface and everyone is getting bullied or having their cock compared to a tiny saucepan handle or being asked to imagine their dick on a mandolin. It's a trickle down of trying to exert control while you brownnose the people above you. It's the system of management that every business self-help book is trying to deconstruct. As a lowly cold chef, you either succumb to it or wither against its might. You half-nod when asked if you've cum in the mayonnaise (this actually happened, as in I was asked this). You get your head down and focus on perfecting the Cobb salad for table 12. But on the whole, I hated being privy to the quasi-sexual half-joke performances of dominance.

The culture is so unbelievably male I almost forgot the female chef. She started late into my kitchen tenure and she was quite nice. The dynamic shifted because the men behaved themselves when she was around. Less dick chat.

Less witches' tits. Less parsnip cock and gynaecology jokes. She was organised in a way that didn't feel reactive. She was always ahead on the mid-service baguettes. A good example of her even temperament was when a more senior chef asked me to clean the extractor fan attachments with caustic soda overnight. Having never really cleaned at an industrial level, I just poured soda granules into the giant bin-buckets and went home for the evening. Like gremlins when they get wet, the caustic soda bubbled up and out of the buckets during the night. The frothy menace burned through the kitchen lino, and through the floorboards, and into the electrical circuits of the restaurant, shorting out the entire system. Customers had to eat by candlelight. And the she-chef didn't blame me because she'd asked the chef above me to clean the fans. *He* was responsible and he'd shirked that responsibility onto me. I cannot understate the new sensibility here. The rationality jumped out.

I quit cheffing essentially because it was making me depressed. The external influences weren't my cup of tea. There was a particularly harrowing Wednesday night shift when a Frenchwoman (named Celine, *évidemment*) gave me my first line of coke so we'd have the energy to deep clean the kitchen ahead of an inspection. I remember feeling miserable to the point of no return as suds crept up my arms. I was Cinderella wishing for a night out. At heart, I'm a showman, it's part of my soul like Voldemort inside Harry, and all I really wanted was the performance of the bar. The customer banter (before banter became a toxic menace).

The talking to people without shitting on them. I wanted to be in the scenes, not behind them. So I left. I went back to the bar when I turned eighteen, pulling pints and the occasional man. And I sent gin and tonics to the kitchen porters via the dumb waiter, God knows they needed something to dull the pain.

The Joy of Ex

Breaking up with someone is the worst thing that can happen to the human psyche, an annihilation of the self. Whether you are the dumper or the dumpee, breakups are foul. You are a Happy Meal without the toy, a carnivore forced onto vegetables, a puppet with all its strings severed. You've just put all this time in halving your world (often referred to as sharing), and then the other half is gone and you have a human-shaped void. The smallest mercy is getting the whole bed to yourself, but it can take a while to decompress from the intersectional chaos of two souls joining. First you rebound aesthetically. You dye your hair Malfoy blonde and pierce both your nipples, but nothing dulls the pain. If you're female, friends offer you a girls' night in, all ice cream and sheet masks, and a deep dive into where things went wrong, concluding that the end of a relationship isn't a failure and celebrating all the room for growth stemming from the crisis. Other women will do the head tilt that shows they care as you gaspingly gag-sob, stalactites of snot streaming from your nose. One of your single friends might be thinly veiling her gladness you're back on her team, excited to have someone to sit with at the next wedding, but this doesn't cloud the remedy of good friends in the wake of a relationship gone awry.

If you're a man, you get taken to the pub where you're told there's plenty more fish in the sea while your eyes moisten and your mates pretend they haven't noticed. That's about it. Maybe a few back slaps. Definitely pints. Within a few weeks of a breakup, newly single gay men always want setting up, but prior experience has taught me never to link my fellow gays. The most self-deluded kind of gay man is the one fresh out of a relationship who says he's ready for a boyfriend. What he means is that he wants to feel infinitely fuckable again, that he wants to wake up with lube breath and his arse all smashed up. That's not the same as your sweet mate who's looking for something less transactional. You could scroll your eligible gay mates, the ones who ache to ease their singularity and escape the hole-cycle, but they'll just get hurt by the rebounding counterpart. None of my lesbian friends have had a breakup in the last fourteen years so my memory's hazy, but they know all the words to every track on *Jagged Little Pill* so there's that. But regardless of gender or sexuality, being single is a muscle you need to exercise, made atrophic by your relationship, a snappable tendon that you can't just do a marathon on. Take baby steps. Remember there's always an after. An after him. An after her. And after them. Splint yourself with that knowledge while you limp out of love.

Some people can't let go of their exes, anonymously checking their social (if it's not in the secret garden of a private account), and reading their old lover's horoscopes to make sure they're still a piece of shit. I do this with every single one of my bastard exes, but we're all Scorpios so it's not like I can avoid it. Scorpios are the sexy sign right? And I'm sure my sexy exes are having all the sexy sex now we're apart (they also had big career changes when Jupiter entered our celestial house-share in 2016). It's terribly romantic to die from a broken heart, terribly Victorian, but I bet it fucking hurts. I've come close enough and I wouldn't go back. Even if you're not a lesbian, the jagged little pill of a breakup can leave you bleeding out and the only option to staunch that, to blot it, can be to search out closure. Everyone wants closure, the ambiguous communal understanding that means you can move on. By revisiting my own worst break-ups here, I'm picking at scabs, re-opening closed scars. It will hurt and I will bleed, but I'm far enough out now for it not to be life threatening. And what is a book of my men without my bastard exes?

I don't compare my husband to my exes. But I'm sure I must have when we first met. In many ways, it's as if those men exist in another time, that they dated another Raven, one who doesn't embarrass his husband by chirpsing the neighbourhood cats. David was my first real ex. A Quentin Blake illustration made real with piercing blue eyes and well-drawn limbs. We met in A level art class in our late teens in bohemian Brighton. He was better looking than me and more comfortably out and I was immediately threatened by that. This unapologetic gay lord who would make absolutely vile self-sewn bric-a-brac clothes that he wore around campus. This was of course incredibly cute, but I sensed danger. A gay man more comfortable in his own skin made me feel fraudulent, a man who could own his flamboyance without minimising it was truly wild. I rejected his fruitiness because I wanted to be savoury. Ah, the internalised homophobia of Y2K, swapping congeniality for badly-parroted straightness, avidly reading from *Straight Expectations*.

But it wasn't just gayness that held me back. I had made the hefty decision at some point after my GCSEs to be cool, a lifelong commitment to a complex system of inaccessibility. Being cool is nebulous, it exists as a feeling rather than distinct articles. Music, fashion, how you spend your evenings are all considerations, but regardless of what and who you know, coolness is a way of being unattainable. It's about cordoning off an unwelcoming cool space with a fairly strict door policy for other people. There was a tribal commitment of the cool to protect the echelons of coolness, to shut out more than to embrace. There's a detachedness that comes with being cool, an impenetrability (cool is of course a synonym for unemotional, for not being warm). It's tricky to be a cool children's TV presenter, because your job is to be accessible. It's easier to be a cool rock star with groupies lined up outside the stage door desperate to get in. In the more recent great democratisation of the Internet, we've been granted eternal access to the VIP areas of the cool. If I've learned anything in the intervening years it's that letting people in is better than making them envious.

But because I was a dumb, know-it-all seventeen-year-old I had decided being cool was for me and I would sacrifice friendliness and general proximity to muggle life. I was so keen to inhabit the rarefied space of cool that I was meticulous about who I let in and who I opened up to. Softening up for love was averse to the position I was occupying as one of the cool kids. I immediately decided I was cooler than David, and though part of me had a teenage desperation to flay my heart for love, I didn't measure him out an ounce of vulnerability. I was aloof. I was offish. At times, I completely ignored him. I was, in short, a dickhead. I was certain that I was cleverer than him, that I had learned the game of adulthood sooner, that he was busy being a friendly kid but I was a cool adult. It fizzled out in a few months, it didn't end so much as never really start. Though there were times we still fooled around – an absolutely catastrophic frotting episode when he and I and his new boyfriend were all Saturday boys in the same high street outlet, and David and I were caught kissing in a club – there was never a suggestion that we'd be together or give it another go.

Four years later we gave it another go. David and I both lived in London, and I had further immersed myself in a world of cool, all the way up the bracket with skinny jeans and a tiny leather jacket, jaguar shoes and a beret. I had evolved from drum'n'bass cool to beatnik cool, my boyhood transitioning to a steadily tormented manhood. David and I mutually agreed on a second bite of the relationship cherry after I begged for it at a bar that sold £1.29 drinks. And I mean begged. I was desperate. With that power imbalance, it was doomed from the start. My guard completely fell away, leaving a gibbering mess of please-love-me and please-don't-leave-me. I was Opposite Raven, the most needy and uncertain I've ever been. I had decided to be in love and it's rare to see a life decision executed so poorly with such conviction. I had buried that need for love so deeply with cider and black, that when the opportunity arose I was overly keen and frantic, my emotions bleeding out through the tiny leather jacket. The power roles promptly reversed, me the soft-shell crab, him the aloof partner. I was mortally wounded by nearly everything he said. I took everything to heart. He told me I was shit in bed. Well, not quite that, but he said that my inexperience with men just didn't do it for him. I took that to mean shit in bed. After three chaotic months, he dumped me in a park and I remember the floor falling out from beneath me, a cavernous shaft appearing and my molten unloveable-ness bubbling below. Within weeks he took up with a mutual friend who I'd had sex with before. I was devastated, intrusive thoughts of them fucking plaguing me for months. In an act of pure self-sabotage, I cycled across Greater London to retrieve my own under-wear from his laundry bin while he was at the pub. I knew I wasn't myself, that this was something a 'crazy ex' does, and yet it was definitely my legs pedalling me towards my own emotional insanity.

Up until that point, my own personal brand of coolness had kept me pretty invincible. A bulletproof arrogance that came from wielding the superpower of being funny. You were either stupidly hot, or sidesplittingly funny. Ideally both, I don't make the rules. I made friends based on this metric and we all understood that being a wit was the only currency worth spending. But the breakup turned me to pocket change, I was minced by the rejection, a full personal crisis of *who am I?* Bulletproof arrogance always gets shattered. Breakups are tough but it can be job loss, or kids, or miscarriage – or any one of the thousands of things that can go awry as you claw to keep your shit together on this tiny planet – that finally breaks you. That sees you in pieces. All my funny and/or hot mates fell too, eventually. Something that we all have in common is being broken and rebuilt.

Breakups are a time of earthquakes and volcanoes as the tectonics shift and the landmass you built as a couple breaks apart. We all want to be the victor, to move on first, not just sleeping with someone great, but authentically shedding the intensity of that last love. We can all get a dick pang after a breakup, but there's a race to get a heart one, to actually sleep with someone on a hundred mattresses without feeling the pea of your ex somewhere below, without the hopeful whisper of a renaissance. Exes are like totes. You want your ex stuffed down in the tote bag where you keep all your other tote bags, his or her usefulness fulfilled, their utility forgotten, but not completely discarded. Successful de-exing is the point where you're not consciously de-exing. You've stopped fastidiously grooming to avoid bumping into an ex when you look like shit. You fastidiously groom for someone new.

What becomes of the broken hearted? They fall in love again. After a few hair of the dog shags with wildly inappropriate suitors, I met Aaron. I've never known someone so kind and so lost. He was nursing himself back to life after partying too hard but actually didn't mention his minor breakdown for months. I had just got back from ninety days in New York and I was not unlost myself, still very cool, new rave cool, but essentially homeless. I would turn up at his flat in the wee hours, a Twix as entry fee to the premises, a nod to bed and board. Aaron was absolute sanctuary when I really needed it, and at a time when everyone drank cider on ice unquestioningly, he was shelter from the storm of my alcoholic twenties (not *an* alcoholic, but I don't think the ABV of my blood ever dropped below 80 per cent).

I think so fondly of this relationship, because Aaron was so lovely, so nurturing, but in reality I was still a total nightmare. I had this constant nagging feeling I was turning into my father, the bad bits that destroyed the relationship with my mum. The way that my dad's huge personality makes it feel like the sun is shining, but then the sun goes in and it's freezing. I was terrified of my own light and shade, and of enforcing that on another person. I had also decided I'd never be hurt again which stopped me falling in love in the way I thought it should feel. I was in love again, but I kept enough of myself for the journey back, inevitable as it was. I was in love but I had control, like cruising on a speedboat but keeping an eye on the petrol gauge. I'd created my own life preserver lest the speedboat capsize. I hated that I wanted to control everything, but that made me want to control even more. Aaron continued to be patient and kind, which made my need for self-protection even harder to stomach. Holding back felt absolutely necessary for survival. I never wanted to feel the fathomless what-the-actual-fuck-ness of my breakup with David ever again.

And when it was over it wasn't destructive, I didn't fall apart. It was like a mutual business decision, with parties going their separate ways, which makes me sound fucking cutthroat. But I hadn't let myself love in a free way. I'd had my flotation device, and the part I'd held back helped me adjust to losing the presence of my boyfriend. I went back to New York for three weeks, as if I'd never left Manhattan to fall in love with a brilliant man in England. I lived off giant ham sandwiches with mustard and blitzed frappes, and drank until I made myself ill (the main memory of the trip is shitting through the eye of a needle at JFK before boarding a flight home).

For the record, I've never known anyone to so wholly find themselves after a breakup like Aaron did, released as he was from my need for control. He stopped dressing like me because all relationships have a commonly understood vision of style. He bought huge boots. He grew his hair out. I wonder how he views his emergence from my fearful iron grasp? After we split, a magazine got in touch, commissioning a story with two exes examining where things went wrong. Aaron was game, but I refused. Breakups don't need a mutually agreed truth. In fact, it's the personal resolution without a partner that defines a finalised breakup. I couldn't have Aaron's truth derailing my own. His separate fiction of why it was over would jar with mine and I'd have to take a long hard look in the mirror again. I simply wasn't ready.

I feel a bit guilty summarising years of love and trust and laughter in a few paragraphs. At a critical time (post-degree, pre-job) when I was all at sea, Aaron had a boat. He was a born rescuer, to a fault, all his friends were on the brink of catastrophe, he attracted them like magnets on a fridge. I, on the other hand, with my overinflated sense of bravado, had no idea I needed rescuing.

There's a passage in Dolly Alderton's *Everything I Know About Love* that talks of the magic of unionship. It's the kind of thing people read at weddings, I've seen them do it on Instagram stories. It's the kind of thing I'd love to write, a sweet-but-realistic reflection on the joy of love itself, but whenever I think about love for more than three minutes a vein in my temple starts to throb and my cynicism starts to itch. I can't speak about the wonderfulness of a relationship without a huge *but*. The thing is, I don't like love stories. If I want to see people get together I'd watch the dance floor at a nappy night. If I wanted to see a man suck himself off I'd go on Twitter. You can't show a female nipple on Instagram, but on Twitter men post pictures of themselves bent over so you can see what they had for lunch as other men approach. I guess, in its own way, that's a *type* of love story.

I prefer my stories love-free and a little more thrilling: explosions and hammy dialogue, secret agents and bent coppers, man playing god and dinosaur DNA. Psychosexual thrillers with the king of psychosexual thrillers Michael Douglas are always a lively interlude to the regrettably un-psychosexual thriller of my life. These films always end with a farfetched showdown between Michael's bit on the side and Michael's original wife, both of which are victors, frankly, if rumours of Douglas' rampant cunnilingus are founded in truth. Traditional romcoms circumnavigate the thrill of a well-eaten-out-but-vengeful wife. Maybe it's the motting out that derails the psyche, creating the psycho in psychosexual? I'm not an expert in either.

Romcoms are love stories filed down to little pebbles of fragrant soap. Romcoms don't make me feel good or lifted. I cannot smell the hope-pourri. I hate their charm, forced like rhubarb. The romcom narrative is predictable, the outcome is set in stone – spoiler alert, they fall in love. Two people are haphazardly getting together over ninety minutes and we observe the capers en route to them finally sealing the deal, the mishaps and the misunderstanding. The will theys, and the won't theys. The hydraulic pressure of a first date that always descends into slapstick. Women in twenty-seven dresses, where each dress has some memory that reveals her need for a man. One of my least favourite genres of film is Jennifer-Aniston-tricks-a-man-into-loving-her: sometimes she pretends to have a boyfriend already because of some picture taken at a party, sometimes she pretends to be the wife of Adam Sandler so she can eventually end up with Adam Sandler.

All of these love shenanigans are my own personal water torture but my heart is not completely iced over. Nobody is exempt from turning to *When Harry Met Sally* at some point in the autumn when the streets smell of crisp leaves and baking cinnamon. I can stomach *Friends with Benefits* at a push, if the psychosexual thriller that I'm gagging to watch is £3.99 or more on Amazon Prime. I can survive the flirtatious banter a romcom always peddles. I can watch the bubbly protagonists have well-lit missionary sex. But I can feel myself dissociating in the pillow talk scenes, at the people falling in love. I believe in a thing called love (just listen to the rhythm of my heart), but I hate seeing it played out on screen or in a book: that when you meet someone you're just a couple of laughable hurdles away from being in love. Love is painted in technicolour, as if it isn't a series of excruciating, existential personality dominoes with breaks for sex which in itself is a series of excruciatingly existential dominoes. Falling in love is one of our grimmest pleasures – all the exchange of power, all the being your best self, all the trying not to poo near each other. Romcoms package love to us as an accessible commodity, if only we keep an eye out for it.

Love stories rarely focus on the part where you're spinning backwards through the cycles of the collaborative history you have with an ex, ambling round your house feeling flat, desperate for human company but decidedly against seeing other people. This sad era is meant to disperse. Recovery is a period, the destination is being recovered. Boy's met girl and girl's met boy and it didn't work out, fine. The focus is always on meeting someone new, on getting back in the saddle for true love, ready to overcome the old things that held you back and the new ones your ex helped excavate. We often conflate being alone with loneliness, believing that self-sufficiency is a temporary bandage because life is for sharing. Love stories don't help with that paradigm, despite scenes of turmoil, of mild moping, we almost always see someone falling back in love.

And I hate love stories, not because they pedal an unrealistic ideology of love, that they hide its realism, but because the pursuit of love is indoctrination to straightness, gay men an afterthought. Gays in romcoms are as one-dimensional as the plots, cast as overly-sassy fabulous best friends. They wear chinos with polo shirts. They say 'go girl'. They're fairy godfathers that help cast love spells for straights. They're like that person who scooped you out of a k-hole at a festival but you'll never see again, a side note in your own story. They expertly advise the main character but can't seem to manage an onscreen relationship themselves. I love my best mate, honestly she's great, but I don't want the central narrative of my existence to be her romantic life. I am not an accent colour to her living room. I won't even settle for a feature wall. Colour me central to my own narrative, thank you. Me and my former Scorpio lovers deserve more.

I'm trying to work out if this is actually annoying, or even true. If romcoms infuriate me or I'm ambivalent. And I'm happy to be pointed towards a romantic comedy that won't boil my piss, please slip into my DMs with recommendations. I welcome a non-haunting, non-repressed representation of gay love, one full of jokes and japes. When do gays get kissed at prom? Where are the twenty-seven lesbian dresses? When can a man sit on Michael Douglas' face?

In the aftermath of a breakup, when the romantic love is doused, I think we'd all appreciate a script to read from, a structure to follow. I guess the comfort of a romcom is its lack of complexity, its deletion of near-constant worry: the gleaning of the *true* emotion of a standard DM, the tricky toilet scheduling. I guess love films are reassuring for the partnered, with the smugness that comes from having reconciled everything and having ended up together. Do these same stories offer hope for those diseased with singleness? A reminder that singledom is a phase that lifts? I don't think women are being indoctrinated by these films because any thinking human can see the strings. But they're certainly enjoying them. They're entertained. The convolutions of real love *are* forgotten for a few hours.

If I really think about it, I'm not sure I could handle another breakup. Richard and I staking territory as our landmass breaks apart (I get the cat but everything else is to play for). I wonder how long I'd be Who-am-I-ing before I can rebuild, how much what-the-actual-fuck-ness? Then I'll be reluctantly back in the single saddle. The brutality of kamikaze dating. The annihilation of the self. The hope that I personally move on first, preferably with Michael Douglas in a psychosexual tryst. That bit sounds more fun, but if I really think about it, I don't have the energy for another marathon of trial-and-error dating with Malfoy blonde hair and newly pierced nipples. If Richard leaves and I'm feeling particularly Victorian, perhaps I'll just die from a broken heart, it would save on the romcom capers.

Floor Wankers

Even though it often makes my eyes roll so hard they dislocate, I listen properly when my straight girlfriends report back from the front lines of their marriages. Part of me is enthralled by the way straight men perform domestic, non-platonic, private straightness (it's not as simple as no bum stuff because there is definitely occasional bum stuff). I know that willies and vaginas are genetically evolved to fit together like a jigsaw, so I imagine straight sex with a woman is like the doors gently wheezing open on a London bus, rather than the knack us gays need to open the boot.

Before I was Sir Cocks-a-lot, long before Coke Zeroes and size zeroes, when Sainsbury's still had little kiosks, my early dalliances with straightness were flatly unsuccessful. Hindsight has still offered no explanation for this, but aged seven, I once spied some loose jelly tots on the floor, chewed them up a bit and threw them into a girl's hair. Her mum had to cut the jellied clump out with scissors. Destruction, if only of hair, is a form of creation, but there was no second date. I once had a Valentine's date with a girl and ended up putting my fist through a window, which sounds vaguely masc so I won't add details that break the illusion. I realised pretty quickly that ending up with a woman was as farfetched as the conclusions in the R. L. Stines I was binge-reading. I swiftly moved on.

To this day, straightness itself is still othered, I've never quite got my head round it. Though I appreciate straightness' rampant commonality, and the assumption of being straight as a factory setting, it's a push to say I have any strong feelings about it. Honestly, I'm cool as long as you don't rub my nose in it, but I struggle to feel like I'm missing out.

Straight dating seems to involve infinite, exhausting calibrations of gender that lead you into the bedroom. It is a courtship dance, a copping off tango, a trek to naked joy. It includes but is not exclusive to going-out tops, jeans and proper shoes, shaved legs, Brazilian waxes, painting your mouth red and your eyelids blue, knowing which reds and blues goes with your unpainted face, clubs that serve drinks in plastic neon shot glasses, groups of men who've been sheep-dipped in cologne, dancing, chat up lines, fish bowls of punch, actual punch ups, the taste of lipstick, dry-humping, bra clasps, the general horny humiliation of inter-human connection, performative blow jobs, asking if she's on the pill, facing each other when you fuck.

I know we're all searching for the one, but I assume after years of this cycle of dating sheep-dipped guys, and bolstered by the momentum of enough miserable breakups, women's once-vibrant resolve to find personal Brad Pitts starts to wane. There's too many fuckbois, too many Smiths-quoting softbois, too many cads who treat women like wines to be sampled and swiftly spittooned. After so many duffs, the dream is tarnished. The high bar for men plummets downwards, past chest height and knee height, past impossible limbo, and onto the floor. The dream of a millionaire, poet, stay-at-home dad who lifts gives way to something less jackpot. A woman of a certain phase might reconsider if her partner really needs to be adventurous *and* creative *and* funny, when perhaps full-time-employed is enough. She might reconsider full-time employment if the guy has his own teeth. As the pool of possibility shrinks, as the search gets more tiring, it's no surprise that some women shrug, do a huge settle, and shack up with one of the inbetweeners.

But before the settle, before the death of romantic hope, before the cologne-cloud dry-humping, before even the fucking, is the dancing. I know we live in hyper-sexualised times, our feeds perpetuating a lookist culture, where the subtext of everything appears to be 'yes, I like to fuck', but dancing is basically upright fucking, so it can be very emotionally charged.

There's something revealing about your moves, very, very adjacent to sex, a fully-clothed but extremely public display of the motion in the ocean. Part of me is enthralled by the way straight men dance because, even after all the column inches devoted to David Beckham's sarong, so many still can't handle a shimmy across the floor. Men dancing can be a deliciously horrible watch, like each single foot is shaking the crumbs off different picnic blankets in separate parks in non-adjacent towns on different time zones. At weddings, where *not* dancing is a sacrilege akin to slapping a newborn, men either adopt the gait of a dozen battling ferrets sewn together in a skin suit, or they choose a regimented mono-syllabic move. It's all a little too revealing, sexually speaking. It's like they're wanking on the dance floor.

I too, am a floor wanker, but quite a jolly one, making up for my fashionable lateness by walking into the party like I'm walking onto a yacht and instigating a conga. Let it be known that I think I'm great at parties, especially on dance floors (I like the ones that light up, the more transient and gaudy and strobing the better). God blessed me with an abundance of dance riches, and despite no formal training I've never stubbed a toe or torn a ham. The closest I've come to an injury was when my left clog flew across the marquee at a wedding because I momentarily unclenched my foot during the Macarena. The night ended with me lugging the wedding-dressed bride out of the water and onto a pontoon in the middle of a Canadian lake. What I lack in technical skill, I make up for with unadulterated enthusiasm. I do not have a signature dance move, like those losers doing the OA dance in Times Square, I am a technicolour dreamcoat of styles, an arrangement of steps that can never be played again. I tango. I hot step. I cha-cha-cha. I render your doble passé. I am Fred Astaire. I am Slave 4 U-Britney. I am BBC Strictly idents.

I once swung across a nightclub looking like Tarzan, screaming like Jane. My airbus on this journey, a ceiling hoop thing, was a dormant prop for a rather classy, nipple tasselled cabaret show. The ceiling hoop was not meant for patron swinging, but the Roxie Hart in me absolutely could not help herself. As a tall, I simply reached up, pirouetting wildly on the surprisingly well-oiled ceiling axis. I felt quite Dita von Teese. Quite big top. And with the natural instincts of a cat learning to pounce on prey, I immediately understood I could handle a running lunge at the ring like a triple-jumping Olympian, but as I swung forwards across the revellers my nerve stalled. It happened in Barcelona, when I'd spent the day in the sun soaking up vitamin D but I was suddenly in the unique position of not quite trusting the bone density in my arms, not sure the ligaments on my fingers would hold, worried that the energy of an earlier patatas bravas wouldn't last the duration of this star turn. The image of my teenage friend's boxing punchbag crashing down from the plaster as I swung off it intruded my thoughts. An acute vertigo took over my being, like the time I climbed so high up a tree in the park a passing stranger had to come up and coach me down (I was seven and I remember the piercing fear even now). The milliseconds became minutes, the minutes became miles. The blood-curdling Jane scream was not in my control, it vomited out of me, primal and desperate, a brass band jammed down my throat like the moths in *Silence of the Lambs*. As with all the best party moments, the bouncers took a beat too long to realise what was happening and to intervene, but soon enough I was pawed down like a Christmas decoration versus a kitten. A magazine later wrote that the party ended with people 'literally dancing on the ceiling', and I've always felt quite proud of that, the split second cemented forever in print. The improvised episode didn't feel very choreographed but that's beside the point. Improvisation is the key to a good floor wank. Acrobatic ceiling swings aren't always to hand, I'm aware of that, but you don't need a Tarzan vine when you're on the B team at your cousin's wedding, you just need moves.

I'm proud that I can have fun in the end of a boot, but a good party helps lube my joints. There's no point having killer moves if you've nowhere to show them off. If there's no light-up dance floor (sob) I prefer a club scalloped by booths with little table lamps that don't have wires. Or a dingy basement that smells of metal and sick. Or a ballroom with a well-waxed parquet. People get quite tribal about music, it's something to do with teenage youth culture, and scoring cool points. You can't get your freak on to 'Fake Plastic Trees' (I've tried) but people get incredibly pissy if you request Wham or anything else patently moonwalkable. There's also the collective mock-pissyness of 'Come on Eileen', where people audibly groan, feigning displeasure, then stamp-dance their goddamned tits off to the chorus. I can dance to anything with a beat, played on grand piano, or bluetooth kitchen speaker, or a phone in a pint glass. My friend once hired a mariachi trio to play

'Work' by Rihanna at her birthday dinner and shimmying in my seat is the closest I've come to God over a sit-down meal.

On the dance floor at a dream party, I'm nothing like those appealing Instagram influencers that dress like a skid mark of pastel. I'm ideally wearing Danny Zuko's shirt from the hand-jive dance, or maybe I'm dressed in head-to-toe leather like a strip of beef jerky with that iridescent meat rainbow when the light hits right. I've always had this dream of river dancing into the Met Gala, so in a way every party is a dress rehearsal for that final destination. It's no secret that my party trick is stamina. Stamina is very much my *thing*. As a fellow guest you may tire, you may sneak out to the smokers' patio, you may wander to the buffet for a few spoons of coleslaw, you may even get fingered in the disabled loo, but you'll return to find me leapfrogging the bride, my battery still at 100 per cent. For some magical reason, despite booze and clogs and overly-ambitious footwork, I am steady on my feet. I bend but I never snap. Because of weekly yoga I can touch my toes easily and, if my trousers have enough give, you'd be surprised how often I can work it into a routine. Not all trousers have enough give though: the crotch of my favourite party slacks has been rebuilt more times than Glasgow School of Art.

Floor wanking is less about how you have sex stylistically, and more about your eagerness to participate. I don't fuck like I dance, or dance like I fuck, but I'm keen on both. Because the night belongs to lovers, we assume it takes two to tango, but I wine and dine and sixty-nine myself, shapes erotically thrown like the clay pot in *Ghost*. I chew up the floor like loose jelly tots. I am a boogie vessel till sunrise, but in a way that gets everyone dancing. The Pied Piper of pirouettes, each reveller a rat hypnotised by my instruments (legs). I want to say I encourage participation but sometimes even I lose myself to the rhythm, the bodies around me becoming a blur as I weave like a basket bin at Heal's. All aboard the soul train, may we all happily wank the floor, circle jerking like boarding schoolboys.

There's always another party tonight, maybe with a smoke machine and a string quartet doing reggae covers, or my mate's kitchen with a load of East End boys and West End girls. I have to go there now, cheeks flushed, before I turn back into a pumpkin. I kiss the bride on the cheek, I leapfrog the groom one last time, and I disappear into the night like a sliver of night sky. Consider this another floor wanked. Onto the next one.

Spotted Dick

My husband Richard is everywhere in this book. It's difficult to think of men at large without thinking of the one I
have at home. He's hiding somewhere in each mannish
chapter, stirred through my life like the currants in a spotted dick. I first spotted Dick (or Dickie) on the night bus,
on another night of shuttling across London on public
transport for a party. It is incredible how most couples
imbue their first meeting with a certain majesty, a beguiling
magic, as if the stars aligned and their guardian angel was
on a roll. But it was just another night in a long list of
nights, and Richard, I'm afraid to say, was just another guy.
It's odd to think of a time when my husband was just some
guy, just tallish (nearly every guy that kissed me before
needed the orthopaedic assistance of a wedged Croc) and
funny-ish (I remember laughing, I think), and certainly
not, at that time, a vessel for my personal sense of satisfaction and a mirror for my shortcomings, a constant test for
my patience and compassion. It's quite a transformation,
quite a leap, but I guess that's the way relationships roll
out: you morph from polite stranger to salacious mate to

domestic companion, while maintaining some kind of emotional equilibrium. These states ebb and flow, but things tend to get less polite and less salacious as time passes, further down the line you might find your manners lax and your sex hasty as the polite edge wears off (this is not a bad thing exactly).

But in Dalston, on the top deck of the 243, I was unaware I'd just met my future husband, that we were Guardian Holemates. Was I hit with the blunt and friendly force of love? Reader, I was not. I could not have predicted a family future with this drunk chap, I did not foresee a Royal wedding balcony kiss, followed by a lifetime of *Call Me by Your Name* summers and *Brokeback Mountain* winters. There was no premonition, no psychic flash-forward, no foretelling palmistry when we touched. I was not enlightened, I was not called to God like a nun, Cupid's arrow didn't roll my eyes to a heart shape like a Vegas slot machine. I was not Rapunzeled from my singleton tower. I was not Pretty Woman-ed away from a life of streetwalking. I think you get the point, right? I was not looking for love. Being a bachelor and cruising other bachelors has a certain panned out quality, in that you meet men in person but never really get close. You never have to commit. There's a personal safety in keeping a safe distance, a way of never giving your full self to anyone, of never getting hurt. In retrospect, I can see I was at my most lonely, but I honestly had no idea. I was ostriched to myself, ear-deep in my own sand. Richard may have been manifested by guardian angels, divined by a

James Blunt song, but I was too busy searching out good times to notice. I did not take to Richard like a duck to water, yet here we are, a decade later, married and sharing a domestic pond, and emotional farmyard.

I remember my twenties as a series of unrequited lovers, the ones that got away, that slipped through my clumsy, selfish, needy fingers. I now think of all the men I chased round town – dressed brilliantly (sort of like a male Sugababe, original lineup) so they'd notice me ignoring them – as dickheads, though there's no concrete evidence of that. Richard is the one that didn't get away – a keeper, a sticker, a boy scout badge in going the distance – but I cannot tell you how and why it worked out. Somewhere between casual sex and authentic boyfriending something clicked, something twigged, I can't for the life of me remember what. I never felt the dawning 'light of my life, fire of my loins' obsession. It was gentle and each progressive step into coupledom lacked the emotional turmoil I'd become so accustomed to. I wasn't worried about my heart getting stamped on, which I appreciate is novel in itself. I wonder what he saw in me, the young Raven full of shit? Bravado, maybe? In 2010, nobody wanted no scrubs, and yet I somehow was one, living hand to mouth and night to night in incredibly small and cheap clothes. I'm not sure how datable I read to the casual observer. When I met Richard, I was a month out of living on my mate's sofa (waiting each night for them to finally go to bed so I could settle down on the cushions). My attitude was very *fuck it*. *Fuck it*, I won't sleep. *Fuck it*, I'll have a Jägerbomb for breakfast. *Fuck it*, I'll fly to New York next week. I was happily, almost proudly restless, but my 'rip it all up' mentality wasn't sustainable. Those *fuck it* days are behind me. I have roots now. Roots are good. The loose threads of my late twenties snagged on this man, the two bachelors were mutually caught. We are now mutual captives, which sounds like prison and it isn't not. I am his cellmate. I am his bitch. The chances of me baking a file into a cake for him are small but not impossible.

Sieving romantically through the stories of the past makes me feel like the current isn't good enough, so I'm loath to do it. I see this with sharp clarity as more of my friends have babies. As they buckaroo nappies and look around frantically for that specific muslin rag they have for wiping up sick, they seem to be hypnotically drawn to the times they were 'still fun'. Friendships are in trouble if you solely start your chat with 'remember when ...?'. They're not dead, they just inhabit the past and I want to share current currency, not relive history. I'm more than happy to chat vomit muslins. We don't have kids yet, but mine and Richard's 'remember when's are honestly so lively, it'd be cruel to keep you out of the loop. Remember when we hunkered in our mate's attic room and you ignored your oyster allergy and passed out on the floor after vomiting in the guest loo next to the platinum discs? Remember when the rat ran at us and I screamed so loudly it did a jig *towards* us rather than running away? Remember when you actually met a guardian angel at a bus stop and asked if you could come over so you weren't alone and I said yes but I fell asleep and I couldn't be roused to answer the door? Remember us *both* crying in South Africa when we *both* got the runs because we *both* thought *fuck it* and drank tap water? (Was that my last *fuck it*? Oh god.) When we first lived together, I remember getting locked out and Googling how to break into our own house with a bent credit card (which is depressingly easy, people. Double lock your door for fuck's sake). I remember getting locked out of our next flat too, and not having a robber's YouTube to help and just having a massive tantrum and being accused of turning into my mother. (My mother is not a creature of tantrums, but I can't be arsed to go into the minutiae of this specific tantrum, nor the specific tributaries of argument and ancient misdemeanour that poured forth in this specific tantrum, nor how Richard was both right and wrong in his accusation.)

Not to blow too much smoke up his arse, but Richard is dependable and patient, supporting my bouts of hardcore typing, long periods isolated and writing, my unrelenting procrastination. I blame my mood swings and character defects on Mercury in retrograde, and Richard nods along, knowing I'm just hungry. He turns the other cheek while I'm checking in my eyebags at the airport. He coaches me through the following morning in the hotel room when I'm over-accessorising to patchily cover my morbid jet lag. He supports my failed digital detoxes, as I try to avoid my jealousy of people on the other side of the equator in better clothes than me. He's silent when my pescatarianism stutters and I eat fried chicken.

Richard has always been Mr Hyperbole: we're always on the best holiday we're ever been on; this is always the best meal he's ever eaten; whenever something good happens it's the best day of his life (I've been known to send him a picture of our wedding day when he says this). And, like most people, Richard's best qualities are also his Achilles heel. I don't want to startle you, but I am no saint and have my own bad qualities (I'll keep them to myself for now). My husband is very measured, which is never a bad thing. He can always see both sides of a situation or argument or tweet, and on lazy days we can chalk that up to being a middle child, a peacemaker. This means I get an annoyingly balanced view when I'm 'on one'. It's a healthy and needed perspective, but it interrupts my flow when I'm about to lose my shit. He's also both silly and serious, again not a bad trait, but sometimes I get trivial Richard, two cheeky girls sewn together at a hen do, when I need a serious man, a politician. I read a tweet from a woman saying she had a safe word with her mates for when they're being sincere and sometimes we need that too, a moment of gravity in a lifetime of levity. It's still, after all these years, interesting to me that we don't always agree, even though I am always right. Richard's categorically not one for arguments, he will avoid them like the plague. His conflict-avoidant state has been known to let things fester, to ferment, to bubble up to the point of an Etna eruption. I like to have things out almost immediately, cards on the table, a tarot of truth fanned on the surface. I don't enjoy arguing, I like to quickly neutralise and neuter the nucleus of an issue before it gets radioactive. One of my favourite pastimes is catching people arguing on the street and retreating to a safe distance where I can still hear them. The tables turned when Rose McGowan (of all people!) broke up a heated marital argument between Richard and I on one of those ornate little bridges in Venice during the biennale. We do, I admit, disagree over which of us is the trophy wife: am I the arm candy of the business mogul, or is he playing second fiddle to the popular culture mulcher? The answer continues to shift.

Yes, I sometimes feel tolerated rather than adored, but I think when the dust settles on the early-courtship love bombing, you shouldn't expect choirs of angels every other day. By far the worst thing about a long-lasting partnership is that all the stupid and unkind things you said in the past sit within that person, sometimes buried deep and nowhere near the surface, and sometimes just behind their eyes. What really hurts is knowing that I would do anything to stop this man getting hurt, and yet I seem to be one of his main agitators, the reason for his turbulence. Nit-picking, scab-picking, getting drunk and being my worst self. He's seen it all. The good and the bad, a sort of potted history of marital disharmony, a series of much less pleasant 'remember when's. I want to say he's forgiving, that moving swiftly on from discord is the only way a marriage can work, but maybe he's catalogued all of these misdemeanours for our divorce papers? I would love the drama of getting served on Christmas Day, I just would.

Unlike serial dating, marriage is up close and personal and therefore has its own up close personality. When you're married long-term, you can lose great swathes of time to petty stuff (washing up seems to be our biggest cause of strife, as is the volume of recycling I create on a daily basis) but the petty stuff is part of marriage's richness. Not to sound like Trump's base in MAGA hats bemoaning the media, but the media *is* affecting how we all do emotional business. Online, we Pac-Man overly-emotive content, slowly being conditioned to respond to the melodramatic – showdowns on reality TV, Baroness Schraeder getting out-sung by Julie Andrews, the *EastEnders* doof-doofs. Despite enjoying the locked horns of two snarky drag queens, it's a certain calmness, and a lack of theatrics, that makes a marriage. I find that the flat bubbles between the effervescence of champagne soirées are where the living is really done. Richard and I live a relatively drama-free life, retreating from the chaos of the outside world into our stable for two, our personal world of interiors, a joint but healthy agoraphobia. As a teen, I assumed lack of conversation was a sign of relationship decay, a gesture of drifting apart, but I realise that quietness is a sign of the work, the comfort, the closeness. I thought in my twenties that I'd rather die than be predictable, but predictability is the epicentre of long-term love. The easy dinners and repeat breakfasts (we're huge on waffles atm). The ever-thine sex that floods your body with endorphins, rather than performative acrobatic birthday shagging. Yes, sometimes we're dressed to the nines like aristocrats in a period drama, sometimes we're talking about threesomes, but twos-ing a 2kg tin of Quality Street in our pyjamas on Christmas Eve, perhaps retiring to the kitchen for prance music, is just as rewarding.

Richard didn't arrive like this, as if overnighted from Amazon. He's changed. There's not so much two Richards, as the fresh one I bought off the shelf and the one I have at home now (good condition, slightly used). They are both the same guy, but ten years (40 seasons, 3650 earth spins round the sun) is bound to ripen you. Richard has matured, and he's on a decent trajectory to being my Mrs Robinson, hotter and older than when first unboxed. The little minx I met on the bus is more of a twunk, and he's grown into the head of grey hair that looked so out of place at twenty-two. I look at pictures of us before the dawn of wellness and I'm shocked by how unwell we appear. Pallid, but glistening with transfat. I don't fancy him less now, but he's leaner, stronger, more flexible and I sometimes miss the love I had for my original podge (his word, not mine). I've always liked the weight of adult men on top of me, their thighs, their bellies. I've never wanted to fuck Ken dolls. Nor do I see the appeal of headless nudes because my desire system isn't based on phantom erections plattered on abs. I've never had a *Men's Health* wank. Richard has morphed out of the parameters of what I thought was my type … So I guess I *do* like slabs of muscle now? My palate has acclimatised to the once-foreign delicacies. I guess I like older men, too? This weird thing happens as you age: the men that you once thought of as older are younger than you are now. It is a head fuck and I don't recommend it. Stay young forever. Suffice to say, I live with a new, older Richard, but in that duality is familiarity: he's a man I've known for ten years and I still remember the original. I wonder if I forged this new man, this second coming of Richard, or if he was there the whole time, pencil lead that would always sharpen? Richard's become both less and more of himself in the last decade, like an accent gradually wearing off, like a seedling bedding in.

During a rough patch a few years back, communication dwindled and I felt us drifting apart. It was incredibly scary and though flash mobs are super passé, I momentarily toyed with hiring a troupe of divorce lawyers with briefcases to serve him papers at work (on Christmas Day, no less). I'm not sure what happened, but like driving in the snow, we suddenly hit invisible ice, swerving across the highway. I want to say it's all cleared up now, and for the most part we're back on track. But no matter how happy you are, coasting can mean less vigilance, so sometimes the car skids and you have to take a moment to correct the course. During this particular skid, I complained to a friend that Richard had diluted me. I was so proud of my youthful individuality and my potent twenty-something strain of self-influenza. I thought I had been somehow whittled by the union rather than fortified. The friend suggested that I needed watering down at this point, that I was erratic and flighty, that I was what the French would call *a lot*, that maybe a little less of that was not a negative. Water, I realised, isn't the enemy: it makes concrete stronger, it slackens a batter for your chippy tea (he really loves those). Richard hadn't been diluting me, he'd been hydrating me. This sounds so naff to my jaded, cynical ears I want to delete it immediately, but it's absolutely true. What I hadn't realised was how much better *I* had become in our 3650 earth spins round the sun, the positive weathering effect of my time with this man. He somehow saved me from myself, a realisation that makes me want to cringe inside out, but is entirely accurate. I joke that Richard's my best branding work, but I am also his. I've always been as chaotic as I am driven, but Richard became a reason to build upwards rather than constantly spreading out. The rootless Raven of 2010 was fun, my God he was fun, but the weathered (good condition, slightly used) Raven gets to be at home with Richard on a Saturday night with a spotted dick at the back of the fridge waiting to be reheated. Couples change over time, individually, and in turn as a unit. I am not 2010 Raven, he is not the same Dick I spotted. Yet here we are, it still works. We're in the car together, jointly vigilant for ice patches. Like people, a marriage is ever-changing, you just have to stay in the car and try to keep up.

Splits for Beginners

When I wrote my first book – Florence Writingaling towards my word count, face lit by a laptop – I agonised over every word, excreting prose like gallstones. Common advice is to write what you know, but there's only so much writing a writer can write about. I thought I'd exorcised my need to reflect on 'my process', yet here it comes again, like Dolly Parton's ex. Writing is circular: the tension of it, the knots of frustration, the eventual release. Writing is always regurgitation of the things I've learned. I find myself endlessly absorbing, masticating, and spitting back out. A bile of vinaigrette on the status quo. Or maybe something meatier and bloodier? A personal tartare. I'm always lightly paranoid that ideas are borrowed or reinterpreted, that my chewed-over expressions aren't new exactly, that they're old ideas dotted with imprints of my molars.

When you're writing a book, reading for pleasure can be difficult, which I appreciate is quite a privileged issue to have. The planet is simmering, democracy is evaporating, boatloads of people are literally seeking asylum and poor Raven can't enjoy three pages of *Gone Girl* without it playing into some existential feedback loop. Not enjoying reading felt, at the time, like a big issue, bigger than realising I'd probably never nail the splits despite multiple watches of 'Splits for Beginners' on YouTube. (I know splits people are the worst, but I simply can't wait to be one. Do you think there's people out there who can do the splits but haven't told anybody? I do not.) Anyway, the dog-eared novels, the essays of hot takes, the audiobooks narrated by notable voices, all became more threatening than inspiring. I couldn't noise-cancel what I was reading, I couldn't drown out the excellence, I couldn't separate my own voice from the chorus in my hands and ears. I felt like a backing singer with his mic off, struggling to reach the high notes. When I occasionally found myself guiltily gobbling up books like Bruce Bogtrotter, I immediately wished I'd spent those reading hours honing my own verse. The guilt was palpable. I woke up in the night as if my circadian rhythm had been upset by alcohol withdrawal, but I was stone cold sober, intoxicated only by the shame of sleeping instead of typing. Things went in, I was collating data, but nothing that came out felt like enough. Concepts festered within me like a shoal of tapeworms. I wasn't procrastinating, delaying the inevitable plating up of an idea that was nicely simmering away on the back burner. I had a fridge of ingredients but no utensils. No appetite. I was blocked. Or not so much blocked as frightened of the stage, of the unflinching spotlight, of every move being scrutinised by an audience. A juggler with no balls. A sword swallower with tonsillitis. A jester of finite jest.

Taking advice from some nicely designed Instagram typography, I tried to 'be open to creativity'. Phrases floated by, but felt like those naff lanterns they let off at weddings, tiny fish you throw back into the sea. I went for long nature-adjacent walks, like a Brontë sister in a reassuringly expensive tracksuit, hoping to translate the sublime gothic into hard copy. I ingested the filthy films of John Waters, a hydrating tonic for cuttlefish creatives dried out on the beach. I did a face mask and de-ashed my legs, waiting for the exterior to stir the innards. I tried intuitive eating and rather than a newfound sharpness of mind, I began to bloat. I stroked my cat, usually a cure-all for any woes. But still I didn't write.

In the midst of the writer's block, I found myself somewhere up the Nile, near the Aswan Dam, on a lounger by the pool of the hotel where Agatha Christie novelled in the thirties. I was here ostensibly to unwind, to deshackle. To distract my mind with camels like a magician's assistant running interference for an illusion. To silence the dread with the deafening majesty of the Pyramids. I know nothing gets me out of a writing funk like David Sedaris. Creamed against mosquitos, and feeling the full benefit of a long sit down, I fingered a Sedaris paperback, one of the few Christmas presents I'd received that wasn't a book about writing for a nascent writer. His latest book was mundane and mesmerising, flowery but precise, confessional but objective. Two pages in and I was ready to type again.

David Sedaris is the uncle you prayed for who arrives on Christmas afternoon, his gift is lively anecdotes you nurse over eggnog. His prose makes me sick with envy for its sheer accuracy, his words catnipping at my ankles. He presents not so much ideas to rip off as the macronutrients needed for book fertility, the pills women guzzle when they can't get pregnant easily, espresso for my own creativity. Like all good people, he's fluent in cynicism, but his begrudging hope shines through like a grease spot on a napkin. Speaking of which, I don't feel the same way about Sedaris as I do about the leathery Kenickie from *Grease*, or Jon Hamm in tight trousers. This is the kind of admiration that would never convert to obsession. I will not send him manic notes composed of cut-out letters from magazines. I will not show up as his house in a fur coat with no knickers. There'll be no Sedaris voodoo doll under my pillow with a pin in its heart.

As with most of the men in my life, it's impossible to differentiate between the actual person, and how he makes me feel about myself. A selfish conversion, sure, but unravelling my return to Sedaris titles when I'm blocked helps me unlock my adulation for the minds of certain men. Smartness is a love potion of sorts. I am a moth to the flame of a big brain, an observationalist, a lyrical gangster. And yet, when I really think about it, I don't want to meet him, I have no desire to Venn our separate circles. I do wonder about his regular life outside the book, beyond the edited frame of each page, but I don't need to experience it, the same way I don't need paparazzi pictures of Jesus between leper healings. You can't have people climbing down off their pedestals to mingle with the pedestrians, civilisation would fall, it would ancient Rome.

No shade to the man, but it's astounding to me that I still like David Sedaris, critical as I am of the broad minutiae of things that give me the ick, the microscopics that jar me. You would think at some point he'd have done something small and disconcerting, a bad oyster in his fruits de mer, and I'd be allergic to his dishes for seven years at least.

We all do this, right? Look for weaknesses. Pull at the frayed edges of the people and things we love in an act of self-preservation. 'It's funny, but … It was good, but … I love him, but …'. There's always a but. The part of our brain that won't let us just enjoy. It's a cocoon that means our soft emotional centres don't get chewed to bits. My instinct is to lean into my lifelong protection against hurt, refusing to succumb to the free fall exposure of full pleasure. Love should be the path of least resistance, I'm more than capable of cruising down the highway, but I force myself off-road into the bracken.

I make it difficult for people to be close by needling them with my enquires into their actions, by unpacking their intentions, by questioning their word use. My husband just wants to be loved. He wants an easy dinner and a snuggle and the cure-all of a cat stroke. But some nights I can't stop myself deconstructing the 'true meaning' of how he operates. His texts during the day. The way he said hello when he came in. His insatiable appetite for work. His shoes in the hallway are a tell that he doesn't love me enough, a stepping stone en route to marital disharmony and my future spinsterhood: me and the cat and a pile of Sedaris books.

Something my husband says in passing can be unwittingly cast in the role of Major Affront to My Belief System. I turn the spotlight onto his performance. The stage is his but he thought we were just snuggling so he's not ready. Sometimes I smack the juggling balls out of his grip with overly harsh appraisals, leaving him empty handed. The signs my husband adores me, that I am enough for him, get ignored while I interrogate the obviously-ominous-and-very-telling motives of his mild actions. I have been known to excavate long-buried fossils of discontent. Everything he's ever done, past and present, has an intrinsically negative net value. And what does that argument we had in Bill's in Bath in 2014 mean for our future, Richard? What about what you said in passing at our wedding? I can see this toxic puddle spreading out like spilt milk, but I don't cry over it, I just get angrier. Anger is sadness for people who think they're strong.

It's not just writing, with its paper cuts of judgement, that can make me feel not enough. When the stars align, everything leaves me feeling frustratingly impotent. Not smart enough. Not funny enough. Not sharp enough or fast enough. My accuracy in the bin. I don't call my mum enough. Or engage in the group WhatsApp enough. Or manage my time like a Silicon Valley exec. I'm not woke enough. I'm not worldly enough. A wardrobe full of clothes but I don't know my body well enough. I'm not successful enough. I'm not ambitious enough. There ain't no mountain high enough. I am not enough.

I'm surrounded by affirmations that I have a nice life – Taste the Difference butter being a key player here – but sometimes the existential feedback loop tells you to ignore the evidence. A hot knife of self-sabotage cuts through the butter of common sense. Some voice in the cheap seats at the back of my brain keeps telling me that challenging other people brings personal security. Picking them apart is my armour. I'm safer when I probe, because the focus shifts away from my inadequacy, I'm shielded from those ebbing feelings of failure, of not enough-ness. On these hypercritical evenings, I can't succumb to my love for Richard. My deliberate (or perhaps it's better to say overpowering) prickliness deletes my own sense of shortcoming.

Romantic relationships offer a life lived off-pedestal, of the reality of muggle-ing, of a Jesus between miracles. I'm not sure I've ever been *happy* happy, but mainly because I don't think that's realistic. Constantly happy is as psychologically toxic as constantly sad. I think of myself as generally not unhappy, which is its own achievement. Keep asking yourself 'am I happy?' and the critical brain eventually finds something to whinge about. Happiness needs a little denial to flourish, an abstraction of the real to distract from the harshness of reality. Happiness needs that magician's assistant to take your eye off the mulch. You don't get straight sets of happiness, a grand slam of concentrated joy, you get minute to minute light and shade. You get great holidays, but you also have your worst arguments abroad, as is tradition. I am changeable, my mood ebbs and flows (especially when I'm living off feta in Greece), which leaves fissures for feeling not-enough. I'm often frustrated that the constant traffic of how I feel isn't instantly being understood by my husband. Sometimes I want to be the object of desire. Sometimes I want feeding. Sometimes I want to be devoured. I want to be absorbed, masticated, spat back out. Mulled over like a good book. But I want this to be bespoke. No rehearsed platitudes will quiet the beast of I'm-not-enough. I am on a roller-coaster, why isn't he responding in bullet time, with new, insightful, tailor-made remedies? I suspect my husband, like most husbands, would quite like more predictability from me, something more consistent to manage.

Of course, it's impossible to be fully understood by someone else. To have anyone keep up when I can barely get a grasp of myself is futile. But like all romantic relationships, I put much higher expectations on whether I'm making my husband happy, and he me. It's much easier to rationalise the human faults in my mates because I don't expect them to serve my deepest needs, to be the pinnacle of my sense of satisfaction and achievement and emotional wellbeing. Not to mention money, shelter, sexual gratification, the need for ongoing sparkling banter, someone who just Deliveroos you a burger when you're tired without you having to say a word. When you meet a lover, they immediately go on your pedestal, and you on theirs. But you both lose your shine as the relationship antiques. This is normal. This is rational. But we all still expect god-like adoration from a partner, the two of you a congregation of mutual worship, both of you deities and true believers. I still want to be a god in my husband's eyes, but I'm a guy in a hoodie on a laptop in a sea of empty coffee cups (I wish this was an illustrative point, but it's completely true). Real life gets in the way of hero worship.

And despite this understanding, I can't stop. What is it that keeps me constantly challenging men I love, refusing to accept the truth of our inevitable humanising? What holds me back from fully succumbing to a man when we're so aligned in our humanity? Magnifying our differences and denying our intersections? Why am I desperate to remind myself I'm somehow other, an outsider? I am a god (in a hoodie). Where are my disciples?

There's a brute symmetry to our lives, Sedaris and I. He is a gay and I am a gay, which people with limited imagination think is common ground. And there's so many people on this planet having sex with men, I refuse to categorise all of us as a single unit, a legion of man-fuckers. Sedaris's life is nothing like the life I've had or continue to strive for. There's the reckoning with addiction, a tragicomic family peppered with siblings, a house in the Cape. But we both have coming out stories, periods in the closet. And then there's his quietly exasperated husband Hugh, married to a loudmouth. That feels startlingly familiar.

Words are clay and I like David's pots. It's easier to enjoy Sedaris because I don't need to be enough for him, I just need to passively read his words. Right there, in Egypt, on a lounger by the pool of the hotel where Agatha Christie novelled in the thirties, I only had to absorb. Right here, right now, I only need to type. Maybe that's enough?

Arsewatch

As someone committed to controlling my own narrative, I found the lockdown of Covid-19 rather testing, worse than my cycling proficiency in Year 5. A huge part of my sense of self is tied up in a certain free-spiritedness, a traversing of my city, the whole planet, touching lives. Sometimes I read my Facebook posts from 2008, and alongside prolific use of the word 'ledge', I realise how hard I partied in my twenties, and how much being in the same room as a zillion people fed me. I was nourished by hot bodies, and floor fillers, and micro-interactions with strangers, all bustling in an atmosphere of booze breath. I'm also aware that people like me, who like a little drink and a little line and a little dance, have a habit of mythologizing their hedonism. To think of ourselves as part of some ancient Roman lineage, some genetic ancestor of Studio 54, our bloodline is mad for it like Hacienda ravers. It might not be true that we're the glamorous figures of nocturnal history, but it keeps us going out.

As civilisation ground to a halt and Splash Mountain queues formed outside Tesco for tinned supplies, we cauterised the good times to stop the spread of the virus. The hokey-cokey in-out-in-out of my social life was snuffed out like a Cire Trudon after a shit, making way for the deafening white noise of lockdown's Groundhog Day. My life, usually a zoetrope of animated scenes, became a still image. Me in bed listening to audiobooks. Psyching myself up for a walk. Psyching myself up for a meal.

When you spend all your evenings at newly opening galleries and restaurants and clubs, where the brand-sponsored booze is free flowing, you can lose sight of how cheap you really are. How much of a skinflint. Lockdown made the penny-pinching worse. I'm a thrifty bargain hunter regardless of what's in my bank account. My yoga studio migrated to an online donation system, and I bequeathed the grand total of zero pounds to body stretching in my kitchen/diner. Yoga is meant to quiet the mind, to encourage a sense of calm, to access a higher power, but I was busy bristling with the daily financial savings. As time dragged on, online classes held little allure, all the Zooms got tired, even the infinite scroll of Instagram lost its appeal. A purely digital life, scientists warn, signals the slow descent into an empathy-zero populous, a corrosive attention-economy, and teenagers asking for Snapchat filter facial surgeries. I missed the buzz of being slightly behind schedule. I missed making a fuss about getting recognised running errands in my civilian clothes. I missed being out.

The thing I missed most when the world locked down was my walking commute to my office. Not because I was eager for another day of trying to be a national treasure – mainly by screengrabbing memes and DM-ing people – but because boys cycled past me on bikes. When I'm walking to work, I have an insatiable appetite for looking at men's arses as they ride past. I can't not look at their buttocks, encased in lycra or cotton or denim. I'm the David Attenborough of pert (and not-so-pert) cheeks, collecting and assessing at an anthropological level. It's almost as if I'm double-checking that men even have bums, like quickly patting my pocket for my passport on the way to the airport. What is it about the arses zipping about that intrigues me so? I just find it hot. That might be where Attenborough and I diverge routes, because he doesn't fancy the wildlife and Springwatch ends when summer hits. For me summer is the peak, the peddlers are everywhere and I find bike bums so hot that even those ugly clippy shoes can't dampen the flames, or those weird shorts that are two pairs of shorts.

Arsewatch is an incurable disease, a sort of heroin for my eyes. I try to abstain, but I don't think a man has ever cycled past me without my eyes darting to his backside. A litter of them kettled at a red light can wreak havoc on my concentration. On a clear day, when I see a particularly good one – think two boiled eggs in a handkerchief – I'm like a magpie spotting a gold coin. I *have* to see the guy's face. An absolutely necessary compulsion, almost biological, to assess whether the curtains match the drapes. I quicken my step. I peer back. Results are mixed. Some faces suspend the moment – ruddy cheeks from exertion, the perfect length of stubble, bonus point for a Roman nose – and some are less to my taste. Not all boys are created hot, some are blessed with good bums and okay faces. Genetics is a cruel mistress.

We all have sexual triggers. Things we see or hear or taste that form a type of sensory acknowledgement, a prelude to a round of heightened sexual awareness, an early, early prologue for arousal. Fore-foreplay. We don't seek these triggers out as much as notice them. I'm wondering how to frame this, if I'll just come off as a pervert. I realise I'm not helping with the stereotype that gay men are arse-mad, I find it nearly impossible to detangle the strands of amorous spaghetti that keep me on high alert for the gluteus maximus of a male cyclist. This is a perversion nestled closely to my heart like a Second World War Bible ready to take a bullet. I've never told anyone of this daily visual worship. Where in this admission of desire do I cross the creepy line? Does my predilection make me grim and shallow? I genuinely think of myself as an evolved human, not a horny Neanderthal. I like to party, and I love men, but I'm not a sad tits-pervert in a pub trying to buy the girls drinks and calling them lesbians if they decline. I'm a respectful member of society, clued up on consensual matters, who can't seem to stop himself glancing.

And it's not true to say that I see a man's cycle-butt and I immediately want to fuck him. Or have sex asap in the nearest love hotel. I do not search out a secluded bush for a relieving wank, tugging at my own gears. I do not secretly want to devour the arsewatch bums, the way 'legs men' say they like legs but they're really saying they like where legs lead. The habit is almost *Carry On* in its laughable sexiness and lack of menace. I don't feel bad about myself, but I don't feel great either. It doesn't feel particularly elevated, and it's verging on grotty. I can almost convince myself that this is the kind of mischievous misdemeanour that sees Supernanny put me on the naughty step for a frustrating two minutes, yet I have a fear that I'm post-rationalising my low-level lechery. Is arsewatch a sad habit of objectification in the pursuit of instant gratification? Have I convinced myself it's a harmless pleasure? Is this very thousand-word examination of an essay merely an extended peeping-tom defence? I don't want to rationalise peeping toms, in the same way I don't want to rationalise Incels. And in a way, by outing myself as a quasi-pervert, I'm sort of admitting that I'm a normal guy. Aren't straight men like this about boobs? And is it my gayness that starts to make this feel off, that makes me feel it should remain hidden? Isn't it straight men that get uncomfortable when we infer that their bums mightn't be single-use? Being boob-mad is societally less problematic, because it fits into procreative sexuality. In a warped way it feels more natural, or at least more expected. The 'leg men' look positively innocuous compared to the implicitly-depraved desires of a homosexual. Not everybody wants the image of man-to-man anal sex in their heads, I get that. Yet here we all are, deep in my psyche, in the bit that piques my erotic interests, peddling in a great circle.

You'd think my fantasy's natural conclusion would be the Tour de France, but there's no extension to the moment of desire, no live action application. Every arse that's watched is a one-liner, a single act. It doesn't need to be made real like Pinocchio. I have no Attenborough-like desire to protect the species, though I'd be sad if they died out. Arsewatch doesn't feed conventionally into my cravings. I do not long to be the bike itself, my face the saddle. I don't have a thing for couriers, sending myself packages to sustain contact, not do I fancy Lance Armstrong. I don't need my husband to cosplay in lycra and I haven't ordered a Peloton. We often think of a strict divide between reality and fantasy but this is neither. It's a grey area where I'm living the reality of the passing butts but it's not translating into a short- or long-term fantasy. Reality can be a ruinous smack in the face, I like the pureness of the just-looking, browsing the bottoms like peaches at the greengrocers. It's not even window-shopping, I have no impetus to buy. In a way, it's the epitome of mindfulness, with all its promise of living in the moment, of staying present. I am present with each fleeting arse and then I move on. Arsewatch is not the first page of a Mills and Boon, it's not the preamble of a Pornhub vignette. It just is.

The Flatmate

I know that students on a deadline mainline caffeine, but nothing keeps you awake at night like guilt. Guilt is the pebble in your shoe, the splint on your leg, heavy on your shoulders like a weighted blanket off the Internet, but bad. Guilt is the upper when you're trying to get that eight hours sleep for better skin. While drifting off, I count the sheepish not the sheep, purging moments from the past, my extraneous brain detritus. Like any sentient being, the silly, dumb things that have happened to me intrude my thoughts – saying the wrong lines in the school play; the time I was mean to my rabbit before she died; there's a special place in my brain for the Amazon review that described my last book as 'reading the babble coming out of a half conscious drunk' (I know I act like shit don't stick, but I feel criticism acutely). These dumb little things are side dishes, I can pore over their aromas and savour their textures and taste light regret in every bite, and that's okay because naughty misdemeanours are a delicious garnish compared to the unpalatably salty main course of roughly chopped guilt. Hardcore remorse isn't easily swallowed. Raw guilt regurgitates.

I wish I'd lived a Quaker life, simple and serene, living off the land, oblivious to my own ability to wrong, my power to corrode. I wish I could have my memory erased like Harold Bishop when he fell off the cliff. I want to be the kind of psychopath who shrugs off other people's feelings, ready to misdemean again. But for me, guilt is a helluva stimulant in the wee hours, and I feel bad about so many things.

By far the worst thing I feel guilty about is the suicide of my flatmate. This is the moment, I believe, where I issue a trigger warning for suicide. It happened in the summer of 2011. And the guilt isn't that he died, exactly, which is objectively, unfathomably shit. It's not that I wish I could have done something the awful night it happened – swooped in and saved the day at the last minute like Superman – it's that, if I'm completely honest, I'm not even sure I knew he was depressed. They say writing is cathartic, but I don't feel the weighted blanket of guilt lifting as I type. I had *no* idea he was in a bad place, bad enough to take his own life. How is that possible?

The night it happened I was asleep, it was a weeknight and I guess the intrusion of regrettable naughties had abated and let me slip into slumber. I woke up, at some pitch-black, unknown time, to what felt like the whole house shaking. *Boom*, it went, *boom boom boom*. I looked out my bedroom window and there were two policemen trying to climb into the back garden. 'Is this your house?', they shouted.

'Yes', I said.

'Let us in.'

There was another wall-shaking boom and I realised someone was trying to kick in the front door. I remember nothing between my bed and the door, the three flights of stairs down to ground level never registered in my memory. I remember being at the door and a load of police dashing past me into the hallway and into the house and calling for Joel. They swept the rooms. 'Joel,' they boomed, 'Joel'. One of them went in the attic, of all places. In the sea of uniformed officers my estranged ex-boyfriend appeared and quietly said 'I'm so sorry about this, Raven'.

Aaron and I had had sex a handful of times since we'd broken up about a year before, maybe longer, and although I know that it's a notoriously bad idea to fuck your ex, neither of us seemed fazed by it in the six months after we broke up. It wasn't surfacing old feelings, it was scratching a familiar itch that felt good, more like spring-cleaning than relighting any fires. I was definitely not falling back in love with him – one of the times he was wearing an ear cuff for Christ's sake. Since things had become more serious with my just-met future-husband I'd stopped seeing my ex. We hadn't re-broken up either. The afterglow of our relationship had run its course, and there was really nothing to add verbally, we'd already properly broken up, our business was finished. We didn't have a cauterised ending, no exacting closure, but I didn't think there were loose ends either. I hadn't seen him in I don't know how long, a year maybe, and I can't tell you how it felt to see him standing there in a pride of police, in a hoodie, at stupid o'clock in the morning. Three minutes ago (maybe less) I'd been asleep.

Policemen and women filed back out, receding as quickly as they'd entered, radios blaring. My estranged ex and I sat next to each other on the Chesterfield sofa and the police asked us loads of questions. I do not remember what they asked. I do not remember what either of us said. All I remember thinking is *is this is a fuss over nothing, how melodramatic, I wonder if the front door is damaged?* I remember the awkwardness of being with my ex after so long under the strangest circumstances known to man. As the blear of sleep lifted, I felt in my deepest guts that this was all a misunderstanding, and I was embarrassed for Aaron, for him making a mountain so big out of a molehill that he called the police in a blind panic, and the officers had tried to kick my door in. I remember him saying he'd called the Samaritans, that Joel had been adamant he wanted to end things, that he'd said the world was black, pointless. I'm embarrassed to recall saying, 'are you sure?'. I simply could not believe he wanted to die and was about to, it was impossible. 'He seemed okay to me', I said. 'He's never okay', said Aaron.

I remember making coffee. A few officers milling round the house. Aaron and I standing up. And then casually, over the radio, we overheard another officer say, 'we've found the body'. I didn't even quite hear it but Aaron kept saying, 'what the fuck, what the fuck', not aggressively or even sadly, just kind of nothing-ly, out-loudly. The policeman with the radio immediately sat us down again and left us in the living room, conferred briefly with the officers near the coffee pot and came back. 'As I think you overheard we found someone, but we can't say who it is without an official identification from the family.'

Phew, I immediately thought, *it's not Joel.*

I'm not sure the police are trained in re-telling you about the death of someone they've already accidentally told you about over the radio. And I'm not sure when it twigged that morning, that I realised my flatmate was dead. As the day dawned and it wasn't dark anymore, the police told us not to tell anyone until there'd been a formal identification. I called my just-met future-husband. I called my mum. I called my best mate. I called our third flatmate who owned our house. That seems like a lot of calls but I don't remember much time passing. I guess time is hard to keep track of when you've been woken up by a battering ram and the police have accidentally revealed they've found your flatmate's body. Some kind of police note-taker started taking a statement from Aaron but as my just-met future-husband arrived, Aaron sort of had the ebbing realisation that he was in his ex's house after a year of non-verbal estrangement, after six months of post-breakup casual sex. It was obviously weird for everyone. Not to overshadow the fucking awful thing that had happened to Joel, that was happening to us all, our lives as we knew them turning to mush in our hands, but the awful thing was too awful to sink in. Too painful to even consider in a real way. There's something about deep, deep shock that means you continue to function as the world turns on its head right in front of you. You're offering tea and coffee and making some bland aside about Lavazza coffee. I wasn't yet grieving, I wasn't yet devastated. This wasn't a survival tactic, I wasn't consciously coping or distracting myself. It was my motor functions carrying me forward before the grief took me out. The denial was not even denial so much as a voice continually saying *but I saw him yesterday*.

Aaron asked the policewoman if he could give his statement in his own home. I was quite keen to hear his side of what had happened, because my timeline of events started when I woke up, but I also didn't have a fucking clue what the right thing to do was. Should I go with them? With my ex? To his house? Joel was fine. How embarrassing for everyone. Aaron left with the policewoman. I called my boss and said I wasn't coming in, hearing my own voice saying 'my flatmate's committed suicide, but they've asked us not to tell anyone', but still not believing it.

I slept for four numb hours in my boyfriend's bed, in the converted attic of his shared house, and woke to my best mate calling me. Rather than ask how I was, to try and figure out the labyrinth of *what the fuck* I was going through, she just drove over, put me in her car, and parked me on the sofa in her living room. She didn't ask me any questions. She put on an Adam Sandler film (not even a classically good one), and she let me be.

Days passed and the cruel reality of what had happened set in, so much heavier than a sleep blanket. I was inundated with memories of Joel, but they all felt shallow: the clothes we liked; the mutual friends we thought were idiots; whether or not Britney was actually toxic, if she could ever re-ascend to the heights of her best hit ('Baby One More Time'). Joel lived in the tiny box room of our flat share and spent most his evenings at work in a bar. I worked daytimes, when he was at home. Loads of housemates barely see each other, right? I'm still trying to work out if it was bad that I hadn't made more time for him. I told myself that I was a tiny part of his life, that we were mutually friendly, but not deep. The guilt of that is piercing. Two humans living under one roof, barely referencing Britney as they pass on the stairs. To have lived with someone and not really seen or known them feels wildly unkind, uncaring. I cannot offer you any proper insight into Joel's mental state, nor, I assume, can the people that were closer to him at the time. I'd love to offer a nifty take on modern masculinity, how men are conditioned to hide their feelings, the staggeringly high rates of depression and suicide in young men. But I have difficulty connecting the statistics to the man I scarcely knew. Part of the guilt is the lack of anything deeper between us, no true understanding. Just the patter of icing on a cake. I did not know his sponge. It's the guilt of not even noticing he was on the brink that will stay with me forever. All my guff about being emotionally intelligent in the fucking bin. Sometimes it is so obvious when someone is careering off the rails (see Britney), but I had no idea he was suffering. I didn't see it coming, I didn't have my own trigger warning. He was suddenly dead. He had taken his own life. We all just had to deal. We just had to do a massive cope. There were hideous revolutions, convulsions of wanting to turn the clock back. Steering him away from the canal where he died, away from the noose. Actually talking to him, actually listening. The guilt of this manifested as a dull weight in my stomach, like eating a bowling ball dipped in cement.

Weeks later, I transported that dull stomach-lead all the way to his funeral, somewhere provincial in Yorkshire, if memory serves. There are no good funerals, are there? Especially if there are loads of young people dressed in mourning. That is fully awful, their young grief reverberating back at you. It's not sadder when young people die except that it is. All that wasted potential, all that undriven mileage on the clock. There was a mild panic as we entered the church because it was packed, and I got separated from my party. I ended up sitting next to someone I actively disliked – a guy who seemed only able to speak to me as *a homosexual*, only ever asking me about gay things, I represented nothing more to him – and him putting his unlikable arm around me as I wept.

Despite the funeral, that motor functioning shock continued, the disbelief didn't fully lift. A sort of zombie grief that propelled me through the trivialities of daily life for a good few months. It stacked up behind me and could not be dammed. I remember my mum coming to London for the day and bawling my eyes out over the carrot cake in the John Lewis canteen.

Six months later and I took the stand at the inquest, but it wasn't exciting or dramatic, there was no last-minute revelation. Just a sad death, almost too sad to comprehend, that still felt somehow inevitable. Aaron took to the stand too, describing those months we were still sleeping together as our *detangling*, I still like how that sounded. My ex, God bless him, attracted so many damaged people, people in need, and it turned out Joel was another man who needed his attention. My obliviousness to that will never not feel shameful.

Years later, after three or so wines, my mum said she didn't really believe the people we'd lost were really dead – Thomas who misadventured, Meela who couldn't get her lungs transplanted – and, my God, holy fucking fuck, I needed that, I needed that lie. This was nothing supernatural or ghosty, not a suggestion that spirits continue to thrive beyond the mortal realm, more that part of her still lives in denial of our lost ones having been taken away, she cannot handle their actual gone-ness, the terminality of death. We both knew it was foolish and weird and categorically untrue, but there's something in it that comforts. The lie that the person isn't gone, they're just out of sight this week, this year, this decade. The harsh reality of death is a moment in time, not a constant stabbing grief and guilt. I needed that irrational truth, that compassionate lie. Maybe Joel isn't dead, not in the cripplingly finite, harshly real way. Maybe he's just somewhere I can't see him. He won't be back, but he's okay. I must confess I still believe.

My Simon

I have a dad, a biological dad I guess we'll call him. Biological dad sounds like the kind of mystery man I'd search for in a comedy, only to find out there was a spillage up at the sperm bank in the eighties and the desk clerk re-filled the cups himself. I know where my biological dad is, he's in Brixton, about twenty minutes' walk from my house, but this chapter isn't about him. I have two other parents, my mum and My Simon: one blood, one bloodless. Two parents who care for me, two parents who check in with me on the regs, to whom I gift my Christmases and holidays, who lend me money interest-free, who I will one day be responsible for eulogising. They're both healthy and yet still I think about their eulogies a lot. I think about eulogising my husband, too. Eulogising my friends. One of my ways of expressing love is to focus acutely on losing it, on the void left behind. On whether I'll keep it together for the coffin-side speech or whether I'll be too inconsolable to read the words.

My mum met my stepdad in a club. He danced over and we've honestly never seen him dance again. I was fourteen when he foxtrotted into our lives, and I certainly didn't need a father figure, having suffered through the opaque tribulations of my own paternity. It was too late for me to have the blueprint of a man thrust into my hand, to trace the lines of how to be, manhood passed down to me like an Olympic flame. I wasn't looking for guidance or nurture, I just wanted to hang out with my mates. In the grand tradition of humans, of course I wanted to be loved in some way, I wanted approval. But from a forty-three-year-old stranger? No thank you. I was inwardly gay and a new man in the house, leaving trails of pheromones in the morning hallway, was an assault to my shifting sense of self. My mum welcomed the excitement of a stranger, the same way I felt when I met my husband, but to me Her Simon was an unwelcome guest, an intruder, the big bad wolf.

Because she had been single for as long as I could remember (there was a guy called Mike around the time I was seven who was fucking great, frankly), I'd long since stopped wasting birthday wishes that she'd get back together with my dad (do all children of breakups do this?). Everything dramatically shifted when we (she) exchanged on a new house, taking us from a poky basement flat that rained on us through the ceiling when the upstairs neighbours did a coloured load, and into a house with two separate floors, no upstairs spin cycle, and a room for me that could actually fit a double bed. Between exchange and completion, there had been a sudden and high key ten-day affair with a man called Simon (we still call him Simon One). He had Dr Martens shoes that he was breaking in but the relationship was over before the leather yielded. I'm sure my mum was devastated, in a way, offering her heart after years of stalemate (perhaps Simon One has more page space in her book?), but she met My Simon a few days later and the rest is history. I cannot tell you the year, but I remember repeat-listening to the CD of 'Under the Bridge' by the Red Hot Chili Peppers because the All Saints version topping the charts was below me. I had masses of Shaun the Sheep stationery from WHSmith. I had my eyes on a Mambo fleece.

Me and my mum, at this stage, were incredibly close. Too close maybe. Barnacles. Thelma and Louise if Louise were Thelma's son. All the clichés were with us: single parent mother and only child; gay man and his mum; mixed raced kid and, well, the rampant racism of the outside world. The invisible umbilical cord between us no more than three feet long. It had always been the two of us and we had a sort of psychic shorthand, a silent emotional patter. I was happy as a pig in shit with this situation, smothered in great dashes of love, unaware that our extremely intense emotional proximity wasn't altogether healthy. I was anxious about going to university (four years in the future at this point), about emptying the nest, about leaving my mother on her own. It wasn't a pressing issue because I had teachers to ignore and cigarettes to smoke, but it was coming, the great un-velcro-ing. Also, a fourteen-year-old man-boy son can't give a woman of thirty-nine everything she needs. There was, naturally, a space in my mum's life for a romantic union, an emptiness I couldn't fill, one that I hadn't even noticed until My Simon stepped up. He was a piece I hadn't realised was missing. A romantic union isn't sex, this wasn't an easily explicable Oedipus thing. I'm not talking about snogs and I'm not talking about dick. I'm talking about romantic love, something you choose to whole-heartedly fall into. A need your kids, wonderful as they may be (wonderful as I still am), cannot satisfy. The see-saw tenderness. The sharing. That intimacy beyond the familial. It was impossible for me to have poly-filled this missing part. And I felt an annoyed recognition that I hadn't been aware of her low-level incompleteness. It was staring us both in the face. Thelma and Louise were meant to know each other fully. The psychic shorthand had let me down.

My mum had been coping as a single parent forever, surviving life with an only child, raising me into nascent adultness. That's not to say it was miserable – I never went to bed hungry; we laughed like there was no tomorrow, sometimes to Victoria Wood on the telly – nor was it idyllic. It was never quite easy, it was never quite carefree. She endeavoured to protect me but I have to say I absorbed her worries. The money we didn't have, and in turn the security we lacked. Houses literally rained on us, which is impossible to miss for even the most self-centred teen. When My Simon arrived, romantic love cracked my mum like an egg. Her I'm-coping personality stuttered, her survivor shell softened, the opposite of a conker in vinegar, she unravelled. She loosened her grip on cope. I saw her glaring vulnerability, her need for support, her own desire to be loved, and it scared the shit out of me. This warrior who raised me had gone soft. In retrospect, this wasn't bad – years of fight or flight energy cannot be good for you – but in the moment, I felt my world tilting.

I would love to convert this into the narrative of an evil stepfather, me the gay Cinderella covered in soot and wishing myself to balls. Most teenagers are desperate for drama, and My Simon, in what has become his signature, brought very little. He was somehow not bothered about interfering in my life, of coming between us, he was quietly obsessed with my mum in the way straight men born in the 1950s don't reveal to anyone else. Our easy conspiracy of two was torn apart, the family nucleus split, but not by force, not by unkindness or malice. Just the inevitable readjustment as a pair becomes a trio. He represented so much to both of us and this shifted what we meant to each other. We had the new stability of three, and a triangle is the strongest shape. As he poly-filled our unseen gaps he also erected new walls. My Simon, the civil engineer, wasn't the big bad wolf, he was the third pig helping us build a solid house out of brick.

The transition from stranger danger to third, non-biological parent wasn't swift. I remember him being very fair and measured and not very vulnerable. He was always generous, and his wells of kindness revealed themselves over time. He bought me incredibly practical, no-nonsense, boring gifts: a sleeping bag for my sweet sixteenth (yawn), that literally kept me warm for a decade of festivals and house parties. The kind of utility present that keeps on giving, more so than, say, a pair of shell toes. There was no reckoning, no flip, he ebbed in. I remember a tonal shift when I realised that if something bad happened to my mum, if she died, that after her eulogy, he'd still be my parent. I realised that our relationship wasn't conditional on her keeping us together, on our mutual love for her. A parameter had dissolved and I guess that was a biggie. When I was seventeen, he somehow knew that the quickest way to any teenager's heart is via the wallet, heartstrings stirring for purse strings, and he offered me a cash incentive for my A Levels. A youth-quaking £500 for straight As, and a tiered system for Bs and Cs.

'You'll be gutted if I get straight As', I proffered.

'No, I really won't', he said.

This is when I realised he wanted me to excel.

When I gave up smoking, he rang me to check I was still off the fags.

'I am', I said, 'and Mum says she'll still love me if I slip, if I start smoking again.'

'And so will I', was his response.

This is the first time he told me he loved me.

My Simon is a sailor at heart. He's a sailor in practice too. There's something bonding for a family sharing a bucket to wretch into as the tide turns. There's a Captain-like quality to everything he does, which can feel a touch gruff to outsiders, but is essential when the waves are crashing onto the deck and you need to stay alive. You need a voice of authority then. He's the most level-headed person I know. I've never seen him angry. I've never seen him drunk. There is a practical magic to the man, cut him open and he's the contents of that drawer in your kitchen with the string and the screws, the keys and the near-dead pens, the batteries and the drachma. He's an encyclopaedia of usefulness, a miscellany of nonsense-free advice, several handymen glue gunned together. You can consult him on whether a glue gun was the right choice, or if you should have used industrial staples. You can consult him on getting a castle key cut in the South of France (that was a long day). You can consult him on a damp course, or the laying of a concrete floor to keep the rats out. He throws nothing away, which drives me nuts. You might look down to find yourself polishing a miscreant boat part, only to realise you're using a pair of his old pants as a duster. But I love the theory of the unlimited shelf life of a possession. Of preserving. Of re-fixing and re-mending and reviving. The constant resurrection. No eulogies. No replacements.

When we're all together – me and my mum and My Simon – there's a hierarchy of bosses, like a video game. It's a pyramid of common sense, that's never been learned, just universally understood. Simon knows best. The best way to cheesecake, the best way to egg scramble, the best way to not use metal on the non-stick pans (I regret this deeply). He once told me 'don't use the bread knife to cut bread', the reasoning of which I've never quite got to the bottom of.

(The essential utility of a bread knife is in the title, surely?) If My Simon's absent (he's probably on the boat) we defer to my mum. Mum knows best. She'll explain the best way to cut the leeks. It's all fine, this hierarchy, until I'm at home with my husband absent-mindedly calling the shots, the shots here being the most pragmatic and efficient way to do nearly everything. Raven knows best. I too run a pragmatic ship, I like things just so. And I know a storm is coming. That children, when they finally emerge, will ruin the streamlined productivity. They'll learn about the cutting of castle keys and leeks from their grandparents, but they'll be tempest toddlers squatting over our efficiency and shitting all over it. I will be up all night and covered in faeces, not unlike my twenties.

My Simon is a man with an insatiable forwardness, a momentum. It's been instilled in me from my mid-teens, a constant what next-ness. When we first met, he called me an ostrich, a boy who'd put his head in the sand when times were tough rather than face the music. A boy who'd put everything off until tomorrow. It's a metaphor that stuck harder than gunned glue, harder than industrial nails. I have been de-ostriching ever since, aware that paralysed cowering doesn't move me forward. A non-ostrich can achieve all sorts (the concrete rat floor is laid, the castle key is cut). But his momentum in me is also his legacy. I always think *what next*? as I push forward. He's with me in the nextness. Yes, at times it's a bit exhausting, never quite settling into what you've done, what you've achieved, always advancing. But what an inheritance. He didn't help me dream, to wish my way through life, he helped me take practical steps so I can live those dreams out. That sounds a bit soapy but hear me out. Dreams are fine, dreams are important, but you also need the tools to make them happen (sometimes it's glue, sometimes it's string, very occasionally it's drachma in a drawer). Dreams are dead in your hand without the drive. My Simon gave me lifelong drive. He made me understand what it is to strive, to graft, to achieve.

I know the world is full of non-bloodline love, but, honestly, who'd want to be a stepparent? It's the least reward- ing gig on the planet (and I might well be the Knebworth of stepkid gigs). As a married-in parent, you get lumbered with half-formed humans, the offspring of your lover. Stepkids don't automatically (if ever) welcome you in. You live with them and yet you have no real jurisdiction, you're just this ambient responsible adult who occasionally gifts sleeping bags. It can't be fun. There's loads of great steppar- ents, full of love to give, and brilliant, rewarding, fortifying step-families. But nobody would consciously choose step- ping, I'm certain. Stepping is always unplanned baggage, it doesn't necessarily exceed your allowance.

My Simon and I were thrown together by a wonderful common denominator (have I mentioned my mum?), and here we are, thriving in our bloodless family, our separate DNA. Between them, my mum and My Simon did a decent enough job preparing me for the world (I'm not sure if it's ever possible to quantify their success). I still call them all the time for help, and I dread the day they're not at the other end of the phone. The umbilical cord got longer and longer and despite our apprehensions, we are all fine. Happy as three pigs in shit. I made it out of the ostrich sand. I made it to university. There was no empty nest. And I don't worry about my mum anymore, because she married a good one.

You Too?

As the Me Too movement happens, I feel quite safe as an observer. There's an almost smugness, or at least a squeaky cleanliness that comes from knowing I'd never cajoled or forced someone into sex, a lightly moral superiority over the *other* men. Obviously, a light moral superiority over not having sexually assaulted someone is an incredibly low bar, it is the under-floor heating of low bars, it is super-basement, it is subterranean. But the feeling of being othered from purveyors of misogyny is real and reassuring. The bad straight men are over there with their misdemeanours great and small, I am over here sitting pretty in a separate Venn circle, there is no overlap. During the height of the movement, I am one of the tweet-readers, the head-shakers, the dismay-ers. We all share stories of ghastly cads and their male chauvinism, their ominous sexual urges, their boggling entitlement. I am *with* the women, we are collectively united against our straight male oppressor. I am on the *right* side of history. There is a clear marker for abundant sexual predatory, premeditated and prolific. But none of us are Weinstein, with his systemic abuse, the business-wide victimisation, the wanking off into plant pots. We are all in the clear. Well, not the clear, exactly, but where we might be accidental everyday sexists, we are definitely not criminals.

There is a divide between the women I speak to about it. Some of them are livid, celebrating the reckoning, the abominable private behaviours made public. Others still accommodate the great male ego and I appreciate I personally have one of those and all men derive privilege from the patriarchy, currently and historically. It feels good to be explicit, it's cathartic. I have work to do as a man of the system. It's not just about sex, it's about the way men's actions are excused as a dynamic of manliness, that our accountability is lessened by way of our gender. Others feel the culture of being chased is part of some natural order. They can tell you the most miserable tale – a flasher, a stalker, a TV exec asking them to take their top off – and somehow still excuse the behaviour. They excuse advances as some kind of highly operational flattery, a prehistoric coupling ritual. They excuse bum pats and lunges. They excuse blatant attacks on autonomy.

We all talk about the dance moves of courtship, the boogie wonderland that instigates sexual contact. The way women and men interact. The expectations put on both. The ancient idea that men want sex and women want love. That sleeping with a guy on the first date is inherently *bad*. That making him wait is inherently *good*. Sexual freedom is great, but if you want respect make him wait. We collectively examine the idea that the heat of the chase is fuelled by mystery, not explanation. That traditionally a man's role is to hunt out a mate, to be ever-ready to inseminate. That women, in turn, should be ever-available, receptors to this driving masculine force. That this is all primal. That we must follow our monkey brains into the bedroom, and up early for the boardroom. A friend zone is *bad* because you've missed the window to snare the girl. That girls are for snaring. That girls don't have a choice.

Being gay has its own sexual rules. Once you're out the closet there's a feeling you're making up for lost time, unshackled by the expectations of straightness, the vanilla essence of heterosexuality. There's an assumption you should be up for anything. That 'no' or 'maybe' restricts you from soaking up new pleasures like kitchen roll. 'No thank you', makes you a type of prude, a prig, and less of a man because men want sex and the only thing that stops them getting it all the time is the circuit breaker of women. Two men should be bunny-rabbiting morning to night, mopping up ejaculate every twenty minutes. But within this paradigm, in my early days on the scene, I made my own choices. I said 'no thank you' and meant it. Sure, in my past there were times I had found myself having not exactly the sex I'd signed up for, but they were all part of the milieu of me becoming a sexually active person, a valiant knight of new experiences, Columbus in a brave new world. Learning my boundaries through having my boundaries pushed was hot, frankly. I can admit that there weren't always clear verbal cues, nor that was I hoping for them because I wanted the unexpected. There was a silent agreement that the two of you were up for it. *It* being a nebulous cluster of actions – kissing, touching, sucking, fucking – with little or no pre-justification. A conversation beforehand would've felt like an Ikea flat-pack assembly manual. Not sexy. And all of us knew we could say no at any time. No was drilled into us the same way we were programmed to use protection. We understood condoms. We understood no. But our endeavours were a bit suck it and see, a bit trial and error. The surprises were what we'd come for, they were the flavour we hadn't chosen but gobbled up the second they touched our lips. I can see now that this wasn't the right way. That we should be offered raspberry ripple before it's shoved down our throats. But the widespread Me Too moment helps us all examine how a dated dating rhetoric helps shield noxious behaviour. How our understanding of battled sexes is cut through with toxic masculinity, and how our residual beliefs continue to protect it.

About a month later I am invited to a party, one of the free drinks ones with a dress code that means proper trousers. I am meeting a former colleague at a club. We've been texting beforehand, and other people I used to work with are coming too. It's difficult to add any colour to these perfunctory plans, it was just another night out. Dressed in my most jazzy shirt, I accidentally bump into them all coming out of the tube. My evening takes a hard corner and changes tack. One ex-colleague, a guy, completely blanks me. I force a hello out of him and the subtext of it is 'please die'. I think everyone senses the animosity. I am flummoxed. I can't tell if I'm imagining this palpable anger, but the immediately awkward group dynamic and the palpable nervous energy confirms it's real as we walk towards the club. Something has happened in the split-test of seconds that we've all seen and none of us quite understand it. It is visceral hate.

I am consumed with a dripping dread that I have done something unforgivably awful. But what could it be? This is a man I had worked with for years, with the usual bumps and scrapes of office life. I wrack my brain for milliseconds and immediately remember the night we slept together. We were high, we were stupid, it was a mistake I thought we mutually wanted buried, that we had both mutually moved on. It was a night that has always been grey in my mind, but I suddenly have the feeling I was alone in that. That it's black and white for him. With rising dread, I don't recall any verbal cues before, during or afterwards. And I had certainly surrendered to certain manly urges. Am I looking down the barrel of Me Too from the other end?

The thing is, I've had bad sex before and this was a classic case. Crappy half-arsed immediately-regrettable fumbles as the sun peeps up at the end of the sesh. I had chalked this episode up with the other dumb things I've done, the youthful fuck ups that you don't linger on, you just do better afterwards. I hadn't been dwelling on it. I'd shoved it all the way over the backburner and right down the back of the oven. And years later, even though I can't see a difference in the nature of this slip-up, it is suddenly being reflected back to me as bad. Really bad. I spend the next week barely sleeping, rehashing and rehashing that night. I agonise over the details, beachcombing every moment of it, picking at the landfill of my memories. The ifs and wheres and hows it went wrong. Whether I was even responsible for the ifs and wheres and hows.

The office we'd worked in was like any other, rows of desk and chairs and people in nice outfits because working from home was a thing of the future. We were employment comrades, cranked on coffee, working like dogs all day and desperate for release at night, for a change of mind-set, a respite from the confrontation of our inboxes. Chemical stimulants help with that. When you're working at full capacity you need something to lance the boil, like gas escaping an overinflated balloon. There's a general unspoken rule that you can find escapism through drugs any night of the week, but you have to be at work on time the next day, and sober enough for more emailing. This particular Wednesday night, as was the regular cycle, we were drinking at a local pub. We called a dealer, and while waiting for him to arrive I remember buying one of those frozen margarita mixes from Waitrose and drinking it lukewarm on the street, my inbox getting further away.

It was all very jovial but we were tipping into the garbled part of the night when everything starts to warp. There comes a time in any heavy drinking session that I like to call Dick Twitching Hour, where the loins of the partygoers start to make themselves known. Something between every-body's legs strikes 2 am or thereabouts and the psychology of the room changes. One minute you've taken a book off the shelf and you're doing lines of coke off a double spread of Kate Moss's arse, the next minute you're all loins. It's happened to me before, obviously, but not with a work colleague, I've always managed to separate the two. But attacking my moral compass with cocaine didn't spare me any bad decisions. 'Can I stay at yours?', I said. An immediate yes. It was brisk. It was done. I pretended to leave and he followed me out ten minutes later. We cabbed back to his. He got beers from the corner shop and I had a minute outside his flat on my own to think about what I was doing. All I could think was 'don't think'. He appeared with tinnies. We never spoke about what we were doing, we just went back to his flat.

I don't remember us ever having a beer. He rolled out the bed in the living room but I didn't get in it. I got into bed with him. I wasn't invited, that's my first red flag. But it's almost impossible to remember any clear motive. I remember the inescapable onward-ness of it, of seizing the moment. Of the perfect storm of being high and being together. And not not fancying him.

I can sit back and explain how this was classic behaviour of his, the lack of any discussion. He was never going to act, to instigate. I'd worked with him long enough to know he had a deep aversion to vulnerability, a way of packaging his negative feelings away and saying 'I don't care'. I found it infuriatingly dismissive, his impotency with his emotions. And here we were having a weird fumble with limited prelude and zero personal connection. It wasn't like we'd always been about to fuck, that we'd flirted and flirted and flirted and this was the night it tipped into something more. It wasn't like we definitely weren't going to fuck either. Our energy was always spicy, always jabby. But the number of gay men I've got on with brilliantly and then suddenly not would astound you. Have you ever had that thing where you click with someone and you sense the danger and you keep clicking? You lean into the risk. It happens rarely and it's thrilling. I had that when I met him. It was electric. People noticed, people commented. But work is work and we were distant colleagues and there was no flirting. It's incredibly hard to illustrate the complex character of someone in a few paragraphs. We spent time in the same building from ten till six, traipsing the same stairwells and reading the same office memos, and with that comes a kind of co-existence, a flow of understanding. But things fester in employment-enforced proximity, and this relationship had definitely soured. We sniped at each other for sure. It was never a power struggle, but I felt he would seek out ways to chop at me. He always seemed keen to let me know he didn't like me, broadcasting it in a way that deliberately demanded my attention, my reaction. Calling my coat ugly. Unfollowing me on Instagram and raving about it at the pub. These sound incredibly trivial, they *are* incredibly trivial, but that's office life for you.

I can't tell you who kissed who first. But we were kissing. He was kissing back. I remember the quasi-drowning of the drunk kissing and a sober millisecond where I said, 'we shouldn't be doing this' and he told me to shut up. He put my flaccid dick in his mouth. I silently blamed the coke. The little voice said, 'we shouldn't be doing this' but it came out aloud and he said, 'shut the fuck up'.

The rest of that night comes to me in vivid snapshots. My fingers inside him. And the two of us, off our tits, washing our hands in the mirror, those same fingers soiled. Still no talking. And then back to bed. Kissing his back. Rimming him. Me finally getting hard. Him jerking himself off. Me saying I was going to finish myself off. And him completely, unequivocally withdrawing consent. Almost immediately after he came he said, 'please leave'. I remember immediately leaving, pulling my pants over my boner, irritated and high, but crystal clear on the instruction. Nuance be damned.

I texted him on the walk home, 'I still haven't cum'. 'Well, no', he replied.

Two weeks later at a leaving do for someone escaping the binge/purge of office life, we went for a line. He leaned away from me like I was going to kiss him. 'I'm not going to kiss you', I said. Do we have to talk about the other night? 'Everyone knows,' he said, 'everyone saw us leave together.' I reminded him we left separately. He looked like he didn't remember. What did he remember? Did he remember any of the yeses. Or the maybes? Or just the nos? Just asking me to leave? My strategy to limit damage was to never talk about it again. Ever. We continued to work together without incident. I left the company. It never crossed my mind that that night wasn't really over. That I'd see him outside the tube and he'd look at me like I was a monster.

I wish I had a hot take. A neat summation of this mess. That I could be absolved of the disarray and confusion of it. In this golden age, complex ideologies and politics are portioned into easily digestible ideas. You *hope*, you *make America great again*. I'm a master of hot takes, and I can't neatly wrap up this episode. No titles roll. I wish I could say the preamble was crystal clear. That the call and response wasn't so murky. I can't work out if conveying the graphic detail makes any more sense than saying we slept together and now he hates me? Am I overthinking this, or under-thinking it? Is it just a very easy conversion? Is he another ex? Or is he still cycling through memories of that night like I am, questioning the consent?

This is an attempt at understanding, to deripple the raspberry of it all as a way to gain some power over the chaos of it. An attempt for my own abominable private behaviours to be made public. There is a hollowness that the memories of that night bring. I can't see the blurred lines clearly. There's a desperation to understand, and in some way control my side of the narrative. And saying all this feels like backpedalling, like excusing. Is this an amends or a defence? I've known enough people who've partied too hard and been to rehab and crawled through the golden syrup of amends to know this isn't one. But you could argue that I'm out here justifying my worst actions. Cataloguing all the yeses that preceded the no. Swimming in the grey space. And writing about it puts me in a position of power as the narrator. I have the privilege to have space to explore it here. Where's his right to reply? Does he even want it?

Maybe he doesn't give a fuck. And who am I to burst the bubble? To ask him what he feels now? Do I even need closure on an ancient history? Whatever he needs to move on is his prerogative, I'm not sure interfering is helpful. Inserting myself back into his life like I did into his bed doesn't feel like a remedy. But it also feels like a dark spot, an invisible bruise in my history. Everyone can see the ripples of anger but not the event. A year after we did/didn't consent to sleep together, in a rare moment of expressive clarity he said to me, 'what happened last year fucked with my head'. And I felt the same. The secrecy. The shame. The pushiness. The foolish way I'd followed my cock across London in a cab. I was ashamed. The sinking feeling that harmless fun caused harm.

I don't think this counts as a Me Too. There's no pattern of behaviour, but I appreciate you only have to murder one person to be a murderer. I think we all have episodes where we did exactly the wrong thing at exactly the wrong time, sexual scrapes with grazes that won't quite heal. I like to think of myself as above the worst tropes of toxic masculinity, but on this particular night I wasn't free of them. And I can still feel the almost smugness of never cajoling or forcing someone into sex, though I'm by no means squeaky clean. I'm still shaking my head at the real aggressors of Me Too. But something urged me that night to push my luck, to be the man who sloppily dominates, who chances his luck, who takes longer to walk away than is appropriate. It feeds into some horrific ideas about gay men, that our sexuality is somehow ominous, somehow threatening, somehow predatory. I hate that the most. The feeling that I seized, or felt entitled to seize, rather than offered or invited. It was his autonomy versus my persistence. I became just another prick following my prick around town and I'd like to forget that as soon as possible. I'm desperate of course, to shove this whole thing back over the burner and down the back of the wall. Did I push? Did he succumb? Was it compliance? In the wee hours, on those nights when I can't sleep, a question still drums on my brain. *Did he consent?*

Porowski

As is customary, I'm scrolling Instagram, looking at pictures of men, while my self-esteem plummets. The men are not really my type, but they're enough of my type to keep me vaguely interested. It is a lasagne of flesh. A buffet of snacks. A paddock of beef. Nipples measle my feed. As do the shop-bought teeth and the soufflé hairstyles, some of which are flattened by salt and sun. I ask the app to stop sending me pictures of chiselled men with their tops off, because I'm developing an unhealthy preoccupation with becoming hot and maintaining that hotness. I know we like to say it's the teenage girls that get affected by the onslaught of online erogenouy, but who among us is immune to the grid of hots, hairless like Manx cats? It raises uncomfortable existential questions: *Is my best self the one I see in the mirror on a good hair day? Am I the quantifiable equation of my muscle groups? Should I divide my body into zones like the Crystal Maze, each one to be tackled and completed?* Rather than confront these quandaries head-on like a grown-up, I click 'not interested' on the posts, shunning them from view.

Alas, that bastard algorithm knows me too well, substituting the semi-nude thirst traps for semi-nude yoga men with enviable flexibility. It knows my sense of inadequacy is more stimulated by bendy men than gym bores. I am inundated with time-lapse yogis and their flexible spines. I am trolled by Sphinx posers and downward doggers. They have tiny nut-skimming shorts and that minimal blandness that algorithms like. Possessions are merely plain props, background noise for doing the splits. They recharge on oblongs of towel, basking in the LA sun's unlimited battery life. They're able to hold complex poses whilst smizing, unlike me whose face distorts like I'm shitting out a watermelon. After my yoga teacher said 'anyone's who's sweated around their mat could you please give it a little wipe' while looking at me directly in the eye, I've found it infinitely easier to experience yoga from home via app, sweat pooling privately on the Ikea rug.

I am a sucker for the yoga content, supping desperately at its sweet teat, unable to drink responsibly. Internet truthers forecast the collapse of meaning as our feeds homogenise the human experience, whereas I forecast the premature collapse of my knees. Despite greasing my joints with baked slabs of oily fish, no longer being in my twenties means I awaken most mornings with my muscles aching, tensed up like an angry fist. It's as though my body has been shrink-wrapping in the oven like a crisp packet, the molten wax of my man-about-town-ing solidifying overnight. My body holds its breath for the night, but can't quite acclimatise as the sun rises, it waits to exhale. I'm mangled like the pre-ticketed Grandpa Joe, but I must get up so the FBI agents assigned to my IP address can watch me bake and eat an entire carrot cake. When I reach for my phone (no messages but loads of new tweets, which counts), my wrists are like the Tin Man's, thirsting for lubricant. My back is a question mark, my shoulders need de-icing like a winter windscreen, and still, like Maya Angelou, I rise. When I brave the hallway for my morning piss, my ankles are seized like embassy hostages. Each dawn chorus follows a sad, familiar path: I must stretch myself back to life, like the supple paperclip who guides you through a Word doc. It's an age thing. All my mates my age are frozen breakfast cinnamon rolls that need proofing in the oven. Muscles that need de-knotting. Aside from being a battle royale of who's had the most therapy, your thirties are a time for trading stretch workouts like Pogs.

The mic in my phone knows all this. It knows my preferences. It's following my likes round the Internet like Hansel and Gretel breadcrumbs. It's listening when I'm booking nurturing flows and Zumba and transcendental endorphin baths. It heard me doing seven bedtime stretches for better posture in the dark while my husband slept. It noticed me in the back of the Uber checking the calories in Berocca, too, but we're not going there today. I have this hideous theory that instead of eternal flames, hell is just you reading out your google history in front of a room of peers. But my feed adapts to my eternal quest for tenderised muscles and lenient joints. The desire to be limbo-ready. That just-out-of-the-bath malleability. Straight after the bath I climb into bed to check my phone one last time before the Advil PM kicks in (no messages but loads of new tweets, which counts). Rubbing the foil of the great scratch card of the Internet, one face always appears: Antoni Porowski.

I know that for many a gay man, Antoni is old news. Something we hungered for ages ago and now we've moved on, like teensy dishes on a tasting menu. The cycle of a crush follows a trusted track. You scope out the hottie incognito, never following, never liking, never outing yourself as a voyeur. You are not diuretic with love like a teenager, you keep this genie in the bottle. But your crooked feelings can't stay between you and God. You reveal your secret crush to your most trusted advisers (other gay men in my case), sharing crush pics via DM and commenting 'would' and 'ouff'. Normally in these pictures the crush isn't posing exactly, he or she is nonchalant, possibly even on someone else's feed, simply reaching for a drink and accidentally flashing a section of flesh that stirs you, on a good day it's an armpit, on a better day it's sweaty. Without saying a word, the DM sanctum (other gay men) agree to keep the secret, a horny pact. But as with all special things, crushes eventually get ruined. More people notice the crush (damn you, algorithm) and the scales tip. Suddenly everyone's caught on. The crush is being talked about by undeserving people whose taste you don't covet. The crush does a sponsored post. Probably gets a GQ cover. Your loin magma cools when exposed to the surface. The crushed-upon is no longer a secret love, they're more like an opened yoghurt that needs to be consumed in three days before going rancid. The crush has gone stale. The crush is crushed. And this echoes my experience with Antoni. He didn't go stale or get less hot, but everyone cottoned on to his hotness and the self-portrait I've painted of myself as a marquis of niche tastes couldn't chime with his worldwide popularity. I debated whether to mention Antoni at all in this book, striving as I do to reveal new things, or notice new feelings. And it's impossible, with algorithms gently steering our line of vision, to have un-noticed Porowski. He's everywhere. He's omnipresent.

Antoni dipped his wick into the flesh lasagne of the Internet just after the first season of *Queer Eye*, hawking multipack briefs with an entrée of abs. I assume his nudity clause was swiftly amended, because now he's more of a herb frappe guy who only goes topless artfully in editorial magazines. Antoni is a semi-precious celebrity, in that his fame isn't in the Hollywood mould, and he hasn't been hardened by any discernible media training. His system of brand-endorsed commerce (vegan butter substitutes, sleep gummies) never feels pushy. The prefix vegan is an instant turn off but Antoni makes it palatable. As we all pan for nuggets of authenticity, the eternal millennial preoccupation, Antoni is experiencing a gold rush. He's a man who can confidently pronounce Tofurkey without wincing as he encourages us to go meat-free. Wellness – the ground-breaking phenomenon of being extremely well – is a pyramid, and Antoni is near the top. He doesn't strike me as a man who mooches round the flat in cheap polyester counting down the hours until he can have a beer. He's more likely to be found post-workout, nursing a non-alcoholic plant-based smoothie (homemade) in a rent-controlled railroad in Tribeca. Everything about him is perfectly balanced like the mobile above a crib. I sort of hate it. There's nothing to dislike, exactly, it's just sometimes, on really bad days, it's infuriating seeing other people succeed and excel. Watching someone thrive can lead to feelings of incompetence, of a lack of optimisation. It's not a neat conversion either. I don't covet the lives of successful millennials and well-stretched men on my feed, but I almost immediately want my own life to be better. I want to see my best self in the mirror, on an appallingly good hair day that could only be described as dashing. I don't want to *be* Antoni, I don't want to manifest his life, I want to be as good at being myself as he is at being himself.

Is that traditionally aspirational? Do we all want a right-on, squeaky clean existence with a salad on the side? Antoni is as easily chewable as flavourless sugar free gum. No harm. No foul. But he plays into a wellness fantasy, a life lived responsibly and easily and not unattractively. His commerce lacks the blatant grabby-ness of late capitalism, he's not selling me stuff, he's showing me the utensils of his own happiness that happen to be available for purchase. Perhaps he holds a similar space for men as Gwyneth

Paltrow does for women? Paltrow's life is impossibly extravagant and aided by mountains of cash, but is marketed as everyman, just about in reach if you can focus hard enough, if you make the time, if you believe. There's a quiet subtext in all Paltrow/Porowski output that *this could be you*. Some gay men are obsessed with Paltrow and her tireless online pilgrimage towards better smelling vaginas and better bowel movements, and I wonder if the sticking point is that she is achieving a tier of success rather than striving for it? While we all toil, Paltrow is thinking *it is me* on the *this could be you* photos. She's not scrabbling like the rest of us. And scrabbling, reaching for things, is the default human condition, our growth measured in attainment. How organic your margarine. How de-iced your shoulders. How seamless your vinyasa. Growth is the modern holy grail, reminding us we're not stagnating.

As Porowski strides through his untraditionally masculine life with apparent ease, navigating the ever-choppy waters of having a penis without resorting to swinging it, I'm trying to work out if his meteoric rise signals the future of masculinity, or its timely demise. We have icons of standard goodness and standard hotness, men we look to to show us how manliness can be done. Icons of the XY. Old school men used to be muscly, silent, moody fuckheads. Masculinity meant smashing and grabbing like Bam-Bam Rubble. Swinging Tarzans. Brooding Bonds. Everyone in a Guy Ritchie movie. Surely this mode has a sell-by date? The masc classic timed out? Antoni isn't like regular men. His app has been updated. He has shrugged off the orthodoxy. There's nothing aggressively masc about the way he gently sautés through his kitchen. Nothing silent, nothing moody, nothing fuckhead. He has the stealth eroticism of domesticity: less smack my bitch up, more scramble my eggs. There's something quite stealthily erotic about his house-husbandry. He's the perfect governess for his legions of adult followers, showing them how to be good men. Or at least better. Whether or not our crushes last, the Antonis of the Internet help us see we can flourish outside the macho paradigm. They allow us to play in the margins. To colour outside the lines. To bake and eat an entire carrot cake, and still know we're men.

Minesweeping

There's a certain innocence to the time before I moved to London, before I lived in a constant fear of debt, before the six solid months my teeth were ketamine and I'd drink cold Heinz mac and cheese from a tin at 5 am before bed (it has significantly less E numbers than you'd imagine). I can get in a jumble about history, about when exactly I lost my innocence (if innocence is the word?), when I stopped circling the plug hole of childhood, when my adulthood was realised.

Not that I've had a sour time of it, but there were a couple of diabetically sweet years between secondary school and university when I had relative freedom, limited responsibility, notable cheekbones and a Nokia charger. It was a great dry run for adulthood, if not adulthood itself. Lots of my friends learned to drive at this time, bored of being ferried by their parents and keen to strike out independently, but I've always thought of myself as someone who's driven, a mysterious passenger, not the captain. Instead of driving lessons (yawn) I chased life lessons, so I worked at a bar.

The Dorset was a nice enough joint, gastro pub-y but not naff, specialising in fish, which I didn't eat at the time. It was sophisticatedly nautical, in a subtle way and not as extreme as first class dining on the Titanic. There were Picasso reprints in gilt frames and chalkboard menus, all very like the Paris the guidebooks *do* tell you about. You could get an affordable pitcher of woo-woo down the road at Riki Tiks, which, like most Brighton landmarks, reminds me of a man. The same street also had a shop called Mau Mau, and a shop boy called Mau Mau Man who looked like a hairy meerkat and was, for a significant spell, and totally unbeknownst to him, the love of my life.

The Dorset was for reasonably well-off adults, of which Brighton is abundant, all left-leaning politics, dramatic hair-cuts and amber necklaces. I vividly remember two slices of toast was £2.40, an effort to deter riffraff, of which there was very little. To me it was just a gastropub, and I didn't realise how good I had it, how relaxed the entire business was compared to, say, most businesses. When I later worked at a bar in London, the tactics to tank people up were extreme: we would turn the heating up at night so people would dehydrate and drink more, loading them up on underpoured spirits. I lost the will to live every weekend while hyper-in-toxicating punters and calling them ambulances once they were suitably poisoned and we'd succeeded in emptying their wallets. Watching the shots you served pour back out of someone in the recovery position as you wait for the para-medics is enough to break even the strongest of spirits.

Though I'm minesweeping memories, I'm not going to record all the after-hours drinking that happened at The

Dorset, but know that there was a lot of it. I was new enough to drinking and the bar was an Aladdin's cave of boozy treasures. Emerald absinthe. Sapphire Bombay Gin. Ruby Campari. I wanted to taste everything – the peaty whiskies, the Cointreau, even the chocolate liqueur that tasted of advent, were beverage conquests notched on my belt. A liquid education. I had been advised by party veterans to only drink clear spirits, colourless like salt, to avoid hangovers. But when you're young, drinking hardly touches the sides, you spring up most days like morning wood. Wine-flu over the cuckoo's nest doesn't really start until you're in your twenties, waking with your head tub-thumping and your stomach knotted like you ate pasta at midnight.

And I met new people at The Dorset, some 'real characters'. I'd never been too bothered about new people because I quite liked my friends and family and you don't need more than that at sixteen. I had met 'people' before (my family don't count). The people I had met at primary school were fresh out of the packet, pristine, without a scratch. University would offer a different type of person, not brand new but barely used, only slightly tarnished by adolescence. These days there's also the types of people I meet at yoga, collectively sculpting our bodies. There's the types of people that live on my street, commonly known as neighbours, though we actually appear to have nothing in common but our postcode. I meet types at Tesco, types at the butchers, types queuing outside the cinema (different to the types outside the theatre). There's the types of people I've met at an afters, either united with me against the guy who's picked up a guitar, or singing along with him. But at eighteen, as I entered the world of casual acquaintances, I was just developing my taste for the newness of others. Now I'd love to say that my newfound love for new people, especially at The Dorset, was intrepid, that it centred on a relentless appetite for their fresh perspectives, their world views, their personal philosophies, and in some way all of that is a bit true. But if I'm honest, I loved how meeting new people made me feel about myself. I loved revealing myself, a personality striptease. I loved sort of showing off who I was and this other new person reflecting interest, reflecting intrigue. My identity was shifting to something more self-made, more self-confident, I wasn't my mum's kid and I wasn't a pupil. Not to tiny violin this, but I had been so closeted and hidden for so long that being myself in front of new people was a revelation, I felt like a magician but I was captivating an audience with absolutely no tricks, just pure Raven Smith. Not the Raven who was concealed, my personality a scratch card with foil over important bits. I don't think I was altogether brilliant at straight-acting, but not the Raven who was deliberately attuning every part of his physical self to convey straightness. Not the Raven who clammed up when you asked about girlfriends. I revealed the me who was the most me I could be at eighteen. Young, dumb, and full of myself.

So yes, I met bar people, but bar people aren't like regular people, much like the queue outside the theatre, they're a type. There's something quite transient about people who sit down, drink, get up, and leave again. There's something equally as liminal about the bars where this happens. Bar drinkers are their own consort. Outside of the haunted men who prop up bars, some of them with underbites, we had a few memorable patrons at The Dorset. There was Becks Man, who would shuffle in on a zimmer from the old people's home up the road, drink two Becks, and shuffle back out. I watched underage teenagers in too much eyeliner slope in, each ordering a single drink, not a round, which is a dead giveaway in terms of underage pub etiquette. But I wasn't long out of trying to work out how adults ordered at bars myself. At eighteen-and-two-weeks I was sympathetic to their quest. Brighton is wall-to-wall hippie types (I've already mentioned the amber beads) and I remember the lady whose aura was a dense and uninviting patchouli. When I was a kid my migraines were triggered by smell, which makes me sound unbelievably soft, but if I huffed at all those glass vials at the Body Shop I'd start to see daggering lights across my eyes. The patchouli customer was a walking migraine, she should have had a trigger warning like epileptic strobing on TV.

There were two types of worker at the bar. The Dorset 'lifers', bustling with potential but only channelling it into the hamster wheel of serving food and drinks, and a steady stream of student staff who had trouble giving a fuck about anything. I felt special because I was neither. I was unmoulded plasticine yet to take adult form. Was I a naive girl waiting to be slowly hardened by circumstance? A stilton-in-waiting? The possibilities were endless – I could be a £50 note in a sea of coppers, or a scrappy urchin – and being a barman, a Lucky Strike parked behind my ear, was a step towards a bigger life.

I had imagined bar work was like The Queen Vic, all dramatic showdowns, sordid escapades in the wine cellar, a body under its concrete. But I quickly realised it's just like any other job, you do it as quickly and efficiently as possible so you can go home. Okay, once some gangsters came in for fish pie, refused to pay, slapped the boss, and broke a waiter's nose. That was *a night*. But mainly there's a lot of pre-service planning, mid-service tidying, and post-service cleaning, which jarred with my low-maintenance position. It's basically a cleaning job with breaks to serve. Very clean people give me the creeps, incidentally. The ones who change their pants twice a day. The neat men with neat hair. I like a bit of muck with my men. A certain *mess*culinity, if you will. A touch of rough. I've always wanted to date a man who plays five-a-side football on a Sunday and comes home to feel me up caked in mud. Categorically no scrubs. Gimme your armpit. Deep-cleaned men confound me because it's fundamentally weird to be anti your own particles, to cover up your untampered humanness. I don't want to have sex with an aroused bottle of Ecover. I digress.

The barmen at The Dorset were a mixed bag. Some of them got a bit mixologist. All sleight of hand and triple sec pirouettes and I spent evenings wanting to rum punch them. Poured drinks don't need flair, in my opinion, they just need enough ice. There was the hot Greek barman, whose name was Triff but I have no idea what that was short for, whose Calvin Kleins would always peep over his jeans slung low like a prisoner. You could see his cum gutters when he reached for the Sambuca on the top shelf which was part of the reason women ordered it. He'd done two years' national service in Greece which was hot. He once showed me a picture of him and his half-clothed bunkmates sprawled on a cabin bed and here I am still talking about it. He'd actually got down to the final twenty for *Big Brother* one year, but he didn't make it to TV. A South African waiter told me 'Benny and the Jets' was called Benny and the Blacks and my sparse knowledge of the Elton John back catalogue meant I believed him and it was years later when I realised the truth. There was a girl who changed into fuck-me boots to go clubbing at the end of every night shift, she also had what was commonly known as a slag tag lower back tattoo, which makes her sound somewhat promiscuous but I couldn't tell you who she slept with. There was a lady called hunchy monkey, on account of two huge breasts that her spine struggled to uphold (she was never called hunchy monkey to her face). The Scrooge-y owner really hated me, he actually barred me after I left, and he died in what the police confirmed to be an unconnected accident while flying his private plane over the sea a few years later. There was a very tall manager, boyish and pale and lanky. We all called her Stretch if memory serves. She, like me, had an encyclopaedic understanding of Disney's *Beauty and the Beast* script and could offer a 'Crazy old Maurice' at the ripest opportunity. She was probably five foot nine, at a push, but her tallness was legendary. There's something about tall women isn't there? It's impossible, especially for men, to not mention the tallness of a tall woman, even in the politest of ways. The giraffe in the room that must be commented upon. Does tallness enhance femininity, or does it dilute it over several floors? And before you start, I know that normative femininity isn't the goal, but the tall manager made men uncomfortable in a way that made them immediately downplay and mock her tallness. Tallness is something for men to erode, a threat to be neutralised, because tall women provide an instant visual commentary about men and their stature (literally and societally). Men deride tall women with witty asides to metaphorically increase their standing. Anyway, she was lovely.

I had been to secondary school with another waiter, Arash, a gay with an adorable stutter. Unlike the tall manager, he was the kind of short that gets you edited out of searches on a dating app, but I didn't mind. I was smoking ten Marlboro Lights a day at that point and I had this niche normal fantasy of us smoking in bed after sex. I once told him he was perfect, or 'the perfect man for me'. I thought this was a bold declaration of love, but he was prone to storms of temper and actually seemed quite angry that I'd admitted to liking him. At the same time, I had a new friend (self-)named Neel's World, who I'd met at a cabaret night that felt like a drag night but the drag queen was a cis woman. It was a short-lived friend affair with Neel's World, very intense and chaotic. He was with me the first time I did ketamine and walked into the sea in my jeans in mid-winter. He was, for want of a better description, too fun. You probably have a too fun friend too, one you have to socialise with in pipettes of time lest you lose a whole week to their antics and wake up covered in glitter on the beach in Normandy the day of your big presentation. Neel was a pipette friend, I needed to carefully dose him. He once went on the Graham Norton show dressed as a vagina. I remember he always seemed to have a lot of saliva in his mouth and a bag full of face paints. What a legacy. Once Neel and I went to a party at the waiter Arash's house but they had longstanding beef (no idea what it was about). Arash threw Neel out and I remember feeling very torn between my pipette friend and my petite imaginary lover. Everyone I knew who was in love at the time seemed stressed and strung out and I regret to say I stayed at the party hoping for a slice of romance (it never materialised).

I had the most amazing boss at the time. An Elvis-impersonator with a trident of spiky black hair that everyone thought was gay on account of his flamboyance, but he had a wife who I remember had a denim Gap jacket (one of my greatest aspirations at the time was to also buy lots of clothes from Gap). Elvis-boss was quite hands-y but his honorary campness made it okay and it filtered down through the whole staff. I remember being initially affronted by the wandering hands because there's a period between childhood and sex where, out of respect, nobody really touches your body. On the bar we were all constantly touching each other up, there was a lot of carry-on-bum-pinching, because these were different times – you could still say *chav* for Christ's sake. I remember starting in a new bar years later and realising very quickly it was not okay to pat a colleague's tush as they passed with a tray of empties. I had actually been out with my Elvis-boss's best friend when I was sweet sixteen (it was illegal to have gay sex before eighteen then, but we didn't anyway). It felt very intense from the off. He sent me sixteen roses the night after we first made out and I remember being absolutely mortified by the public display of affection. He was fun though, basically because he let me drink indoors which is tricky to accomplish at sixteen, but on reflection feels more *cool mom* than boyfriend. Dating my boss's best mate was a novel way to understand the adage: don't shit where you eat. Because I was a mid-teenager with a casual disregard for other people's feelings, I didn't really break up with the guy so much as ghost him (it wasn't called that then). It wasn't meant to be malicious, I don't think, I just literally had no emotional equipment to let him down gently. He's not in a brilliant place now, I think the booze got the better of him. But he was lovely to me before I solidified into dreadful adulthood and that constant fear of debt got purchase. He lived above a crêperie, oddly, and his little flat was wall-to-wall photography books. I remember thinking he was amazing because he had the same Habitat sofas they had in the *Big Brother* house (I am cringing off my chair at this memory). We'd sit on his *Big Brother* sofa and drink wine indoors, which at the time was all I needed.

The Graduate

I once got hit in the face with an orange, assaulted with a citrus fruit if you will. It wasn't on purpose, but it still hurt.

It was at a birthday drinks around the time of the London Olympics, in a bar on Ridley Road Market in East London. The bar may well still be there, and it probably has a circular blue plaque that says 'Raven Smith got Tangoed here'. It was a grubby little place, with toilets that still feel like outhouses, remnants from Victorian London with chipped tiles and non-existent heat so you can see the steam rise off your piss. The bar's décor was sourced entirely from the market itself, which is a nice idea because the gentrifying masses love a touch of community with their hedonism, but you also end up with two plastic colanders masquerading as a lampshade. You could see the bare bulb through the holes and traces of light danced on your eyeballs after you looked away. It compounded any drunkenness and wasn't altogether pleasant.

I'd love to ground this time period in critical world events but my addiction to the Internet's deathless scroll was burgeoning and I only remember a few things – the lady who put the cat in the bin; the Spanish woman who grievously retouched a Jesus fresco, smudging it out of recognition (I think about this whenever I get a bit sad and it helps); the British woman who hit her head and got a 'Chinese' accent; Frank Ocean coming out on Tumblr. Samantha Brick saying she was insatiably hot happened somewhere in the mix here too, as was 'two girls, one cup', but I'm patchy on dates. On reflection, this may have been the greatest epoch in the history of the trivial Internet, where brilliant stories lasted days rather than minutes and there were no memes.

It was someone's birthday because it's always someone's birthday and we, in our roaring twenties, needed cover stories to heavily drink. All of us getting out of our skulls on cheap drinks, trying to delete the noise of our entry-level jobs, alcohol waterproofing us against reality. When you're a student, especially in London, every night is one for cheap drinks; the big, mad-for-it Fridays and Saturdays are irrelevant because you're out whenever you want. Clubs reel you in with the maggot of cheap drinks, kettling you on a dance floor for bops with just the right amount of cheese. You're never not binge drinking with likeminded idiots. There's no weekend, no week either really, just a slurred series of evenings. Anything is possible. Go to G-A-Y Late on a weeknight, with its drink deals and mainstream faggotry. Get ejected from G-A-Y Late later that same weeknight and mott out on a falafel pita on the night bus. Get up tomorrow and do it again.

When you hit early adulthood as graduates, and enter workplaces with rigorous timeframes, Fridays become the finale of the juggernaut that is the capitalist working week. That particular period of early-employment was punctuated by metallic brogues, Cambridge satchels, cronuts, and the cereal café on Brick Lane. Work itself is a culture shock from the general malaise of studenthood. You suddenly have mornings with a routine that gets you out of the house and onto a tube and into an office. You spend your earliest career days trying not to get caught Googling how to do the tasks you said you were proficient at on your CV, but you do acclimatise. Offices, often in achingly openly planned spaces, have a culture you slowly adapt to, you sort of absorb the local customs like they're nicotine patched onto your skin.

Each person I've met on this planet carries a delicious individualism, snowflaked as human life is, but they can also be categorised into certain types, sorted into larger houses. At work these types get shoved together in a great vocational jambalaya, all your icky humanness smooshed while you try and achieve a communal task. There's brown-nosers, there's always brown-nosers. Hard-boiled brown-nosers with Machiavellian tendencies, scurrying round after the big boss. There's always someone with head girl energy, but they needn't be a girl, nor particularly advanced up the chain. There's always someone who's desperately trying to get outside-of-work events happening, pleading for a night at the pub or, God forbid, bowling. There's someone who willingly lets their hangover pollute the whole space, fumigating the room until everyone agrees to get pizzas Pollock-ed with pepperoni for lunch. There's someone who's perennially late like it's a personality trait (it's not). Someone who calls in sick at the slightest sniffle (I had a colleague who didn't come in one day because her cat got in a fight with another cat, but I think that was more indicative of some trickle down bullying). Someone (like me) who chats in a distracting way but still does all their work. The guys that run accounts aren't a universal type exactly, but you'd be smart to keep them onside at all costs: they take so much shit from people chasing invoices that the tiniest morsel of friendship keeps the wheels greased and your own suppliers getting paid.

And you have a collective history in a workspace. Silly spats that congeal in the room like Boxing Day bread sauce, forming into a crust of ancient grudge. People conspire against each other, chasing credit and affirmation from the boss. There's always someone to curb your procrastination, or ask why you're in a mood (nothing puts me in a mood like being asked why I'm in a mood). Offices have a needy co-worker co-dependence, coupled with constant one-up-manship, everyone with an eye on a promotion. There's lots of people who work hard but don't make a big thing of it. There's people who work hard and like to point it out at every opportunity. There's people who don't really work hard but seem to get constantly rewarded. All of this feeds into the congealing bread sauce of spats, the Montague versus Capulet grudges. Some bosses like to insinuate a team is like a family of kinfolk, but we've yet to fire my gun-toting, possibly-racist uncle from The Smiths. As a newbie in the room it's all quite fun, quite entertaining, apart from that in order to be valid and un-fireable, you have to dig your own fingers into your own dirt patch, driving a stake into your own miserable square of land and yield a crop for your boss. Your Neanderthal fight or flight reflexes – evolved to armour you from a sabre-toothed tiger or cranky woolly mammoth – are channelled into spreadsheets and Word docs that imply your ownership of tasks, that safeguard your own ideas. There's a monthly cycle in an office too. I'm not talking about women syncing up, but rather the more equally-gendered conundrum of too much month at the end of your money. Everyone supplementing their financial wellbeing with a Monzo overdraft, drinking nothing but soup as payday inches closer. Actually, there's always one excruciatingly rich intern who eats well throughout their tenure. They wear The Row.

I can't shake the feeling that office-life is fundamentally toxic, the ingrained hierarchy corrosive to reasonable human growth. But you can hate the hierarchy of a place and still scale it (oh God, I think capitalism works like this too, but this isn't the time). Nearly every job I've had has come with reams of male privilege. I found myself carving out a niche as the naughty-but-promising boy in an office of women. Naughtiness is more tolerated in men to be honest. I was still listened to in meetings. I did once get accused of mansplaining (I'm fucking certain I wasn't), but most of the time men are listened to regardless of skill or accuracy. I have a filthy habit of turning the air loud, and I'm brash and unapologetically confident and I wonder how many of the women I worked with were allowed those qualities in the same quantities? Some of my female colleagues would sort of unsay things they'd said, a quiet 'or not' at the end of anything that could be deemed direct, a lightly passive disclaimer after an assertive act.

My job at the time was entry-level, despite already being five years out of university. Post higher education, I'd had my first lucky break, transitioning from intern with an asymmetric haircut (even I'm not sure how I managed that), to art books editor. The schedule was demanding (I oversaw seven titles the year I was there), and as a youngster entering the industry I didn't realise the power of taking any type of break. I was anti-downtime. I just grafted harder and harder like Boxer in *Animal Farm*, not getting more efficient or strengthening my concentration, because I was fighting a bone tiredness that never lifted. My boss was a nightmare, frankly, the kind of man who presented as quite bohemian and architectural, but had a nasty habit of barking at people, of deliberately making them feel small. People were genuinely terrified of him, and I remember lots of tears in meetings and genuinely stunned silences. A freelance designer once lost the physical draft of a book and was publicly flogged, well, flogged with words. It sounds like a toxic workplace because it was. As a survivor, a cockroach of the workplace, I very quickly mastered the key skill to any working life: disarmament. I repeatedly and systematically disarmed my boss. I've never had to nullify a rising anger quite like I did in that job. I'm not completely sure how I did it. While others wriggled and winced from his verbal assaults, I somehow slid forward unharmed. I never once got in trouble (until the day he finally exploded and demoted everyone on the staff and I slipped my resignation under his hand before he had a chance to bin me off).

So yeah, if you're one of the graduates lucky enough to be dropped into adult employment, Fridays are your respite, an escape from the chess game of office politics. Fridays are the blurred line between the working week and wanton playtime. It can be difficult to change your mind-set from work to fun but the best catalyst is booze. The thing is, that even as a rampant drinker, I'm not really one for pubs. I find them a bit cosy, a bit blah. I'd rather watch paint dry than nestle on a velvety banquette with a pint. Pubs just feels a bit drab, a bit dormant. I'm a stand-up drunk, I like to shimmy. It's the queuing in pubs that really gets on my tits and under my skin. Just as you start to relax it's your round and you have to get back up and order. I'm not a pretty girl, you see, and pretty girls get served swiftly. They get the attention that segues into attentive service and carbonated beverages. I can tip a fiver every goddamn round and still get ignored in a sea of customers. I love a bar, though, preferably with stools screwed to the floor and little hooks by your knees, where people lean over you to order, their armpit your temporary accommodation. Something about sitting at a bar is closer to standing and that comforts me, like I'm not sinking into my night, that my core strength has some utility. In a way, sitting at the bar is stationary queueing, the type I can manage. Sitting at a bar, you *are* the queue, you never have to join it from the rear, the backs of pretty girls' heads your world view, hoping the barman noticed that fiver you tipped. Just today I was calling for more bars. Wine bars. Cocktail bars. Hotel bars. The counter at a diner. Diners are a different ballgame, because they also serve pie (you should always eat it crust-to-point and make a wish on the final tip fyi).

Back to the orange assault, for we have digressed a little. On that literally fruitful night, at the bar on the market with the colander lampshades, we gathered like bobbing Halloween apples, glasses of beer or gin and tonic thrown down the neck. The look of the time was horse girl. A Breton and a Barbour; a messy pony (your hair, not your livestock); an off-duty model in the countryside energy, a sniff of metropolitan life but ever-ready to muck in (or muck out). I wasn't above the horseplay. I had a waxen jacket and innumerable stripy tops but I have never worn wellingtons in the city, that has always struck me as a step too far, even on the rainiest of commutes. I look back at pictures from the time but they were all taken on a blackberry, the forgiving pixilation obscuring the closer details of the deranged fits. I'm sorry I can't be more gentle with this, but I looked cheap. I was kind of raggedy in appearance. Nothing looked finished or fitted, let alone pricey. Entry-level jobs lack the paycheque that gets you to glossy and glamorous and expensive, but luckily there's an abundance of horse girl attire in charity shops, a surplus. Yet despite our equestrian tendencies, we were all distinctly urban, listening exclusively to Beyoncé, once even venturing (everything's a schlep when you're skint) to the Millennium Dome to see her live. We won the golden tickets doing karaoke in a dive bar in Soho, and took a boat which felt particularly schleppy. It was the chaotic post *Single Ladies*-Sasha Fierce era, and we had to sit through a miserable orchestral rendition of 'If I Were a Boy'. There was a period when slut dropping was 'the thing we all did', ironically at first and then, once mastered, whenever we felt like it. Slut drops punctuated our evenings, especially encouraged between rounds of market beer. Waking with the ironclad knees and brittle leg joints after a night of slut dropping is something that everyone has to experience at least once.

In East London, as the sluts dropped, I went outside for a cigarette because I was still a smoker, because at that point smoking had yet to tip from carelessly unhealthy to fucking disgusting. A very drunk friend of a friend was in the smoking pen (a square of market drawn in spray paint outside the bar) yammering on about something inane. He seemed on the verge of blackout, or perhaps had already entered that fateful stage of drunkenness and was zombie-ing blithely onward. As I turned to re-enter the market bar, he picked up an orange and threw it. Sort of at nobody, sort of at the bar. The citrus orb hit me square in the face: nose first, then cheeks. Drunk people do strange things, their bravado peaking, their inhibitions mush. I can't be bothered to assign some meaning to the orange lob, but based on the action alone, may I just say for the record that the guy was a clownshoe.

Have you ever got out of the bath and had the taps scrape your back, forking at your naked skin? It doesn't hurt immediately, it's not painful, it's just the time before the pain hits when you know it's coming, it's anticipation. Getting hit in the face with an orange is the opposite of taps in the bath. The pain was instant and opaque, a lava of boiling Tropicana poured directly onto my face. I guess people who get punched all the time are used to this sensation of thuddery, but as a sporadic punchee I was stunned, grappling for meaning. I thought my eyes would pop from their sockets and dribble to my chin on veiny stalks. I felt my face for blood, but my fingers came back clean, my eyeballs hadn't moved. A reactive heaving mouth-breathing ensued. My nose was pins, my lips needles, the guy was gone. I don't know if you've ever had someone throw something into your face as hard as they can, but I fully understand why cricketers wear cups. It doesn't matter what kind of working week you've had, how much gin you've consumed, how striped your Breton, how messy your pony, an orange to the face is immediately sobering. As the buoyant ABV blood in my veins turned to lead, I walked back into the bar for another drink, a restorative toddy to de-orange my nerves. Nothing gets between me and the Friday night crossover. The weekend was just beginning and it was my round.

Dangerous Liaisons

It's usually an unprecedented horniness that gets you back on the market after a breakup, but casual sex only stretches so far before the elastic gets taut. After the bit when your heart's brittle like cold-day toffee, after you've listened to your song until your ears bleed, after you cry-puke in the toilets of a pub on a Saturday afternoon, after you decide your ex is criminally insane, you're ready to pound-coin the foil off the scratch card of romantic possibility. You realise, slightly begrudgingly, that you're ready for love again, which is possibly a Donna Summer song. Like a glamour girl leaving *I'm a Celebrity*, you're ready for the next chapter. You're ready for anniversaries rather than 'u up?' texts; for the masturbation to be mutual, communal even; for someone to make love to you, not just your holes.

There are so many different ways to fall in love: head over heels or arse over tit. And personal readiness doesn't always convert into a relationship. You can be open to the universe 'giving you love', your heart un-ziplocked and defrosting. You can be single but self-actualising, saying affirmations in the mirror like Candyman and right-swiping your tits off.

You can be actively window shopping suitors with the zeal of Sonic getting rings. But the stars staunchly refuse to align. It just doesn't go to plan. Love, regrettably, is a game of chance, and rolling the dice doesn't always get you a Yahtzee. The likelihood of falling in love, of finding someone to love you back, doesn't instantaneously quadruple because you're wearing nice pants and waxing full time. They energy it takes to be new-shag-ready 24/7 is so exhausting that you're bound to slip. There'll be nights where you take your eye off the ball, diverting your attention entirely to the champagne and trays of those fiddly sandwiches held together with little sticks. You'll feel woozy and free and something in your pants will stir. This is when you'll bump into a charming prince, possibly The One, but you're too horny, like Mousse T. horny, and you ruin it all with your urges.

I was, initially, quite comfortable in the no man's land of being single, in the abyss of sexual penury, in dick poverty. I was neither furiously rutting strangers on days with a y, nor settling down with a decent chap (decent chaps like to furiously rut too). I was a perennial fuckboy-in-waiting, lacking whatever special sauce it takes to have a string of eligible bachelors in my DMs. I have a habit of making men nervous, which isn't great for obtaining and sustaining erections (them, not me). But I was still keen on trial and error-ing boyfriends, and I did meet a few men of note. There was the neighbour who ate my arse in such an exquisite way I wanted to write poetry, but I didn't like his home décor, especially a rather nasty desk where one assumes he sat perfecting his analingus on a peach, so I gently stopped responding to his messages. I had a few dates with a man called Ben who'd had a stroke and couldn't get it up (not sure if that was a correlation). Younger men are always eager to fuck, very enthusiastic, but they're not, on the whole, brilliant at it. They seem so excited to have their mouth on your dick that they either neglect to follow up with any discernible technique, or rip something off from porn that's hugely aggressive and doesn't feel nice. Men, like snowflakes, are all different. You can find yourself going through the motions with a man as he half dissociates, and has sex with the component parts of your body like he's painting by numbers. You're together but he's not *there*, not really. These men treat nearly everything as a pit stop to penetrative sex, a perfunctory action, almost mindless, like rinsing a glass before you put it in the dishwasher. At this point I'd like to say thank you to my neighbour for realising that my bumhole isn't an entrée, it's not a snack, it's a whole damn meal. Who are my other regrettable fumbles? Oh, the guy who ran a club night I loved in a working men's club, and came home with me and then suddenly froze and left. I only got to the bottom of it twenty years later when a mutual friend said he'd seen the posters of his night on the wall and told everybody I was obsessed with him (I'm still livid, frankly). There was the guy who told me he was in love with his best mate who was also his flatmate and was sort of spying on him, which terminated my desire instantaneously. And further back, before I could even hold my alcohol, I met dozens of men who didn't fit the bill, not quite. Guys in liberal outfits, underlaid with Tory underwear. Rich boys who spoke with an affected I'm-not-rich lilt like Bert from *Mary Poppins*. I've dated some under-evolved men, I've had a few trogla-dates. I once made out with a man who was essentially a balloon on a stick with a smiley face drawn on. One guy was nothing more than a sentient Babybel.

There's something about reality that's always let me down. And I've found myself over the years, enjoying the ambient idea of a passionate relationship with people I don't quite know, the fantasy shags, rather than the precise reality of the men. Earlier on in my relationship with my now-husband, these intensive fantasies about other men terrified me with their white-hot obsession. I assumed that they had some meaning, proved something was missing at home. But my crushes, for crushes they were, always fizzled out, they never found purchase. It was the danger of the fantasy infidelity that I loved, not the actual infidelity. And rather than berate myself for this grass-is-greener parallel fantasy life, I now indulge in it. It is harmless, it never converts to an actionable list, nor would I want it to. It's an impossibly hot fantasy precisely because it's impossible. We all do this (I hope). I don't think we fantasise about real life, it defeats the point because there's something a bit unhorny about over-familiarity. It's still erotic in its own way at home, but it doesn't match the fantasy of a fantasy, that's why the fantasy is needed. I don't think we masturbate over our partners, over the comforts of the existences we already inhabit. I've yet to finish myself off to a shepherd's pie and a back rub, lovely as they are. We wank for implausible couplings, for impossible conquests, for dangerous liaisons.

There's a guy I barely know who lives in New York. Let's call him Peter (Peter is his name). Peter and I have been DM-ing so long I can't remember who started it. We're talking maybe seven years. I don't wank over Peter – though I'm sure he understands my arse's not an entrée – because the fantasy is much more domestic. I'm certain I'd be married to him if I wasn't with my husband, though Peter's never given any suggestion he liked me back, never hinted we're anything more than sassy-commenting DM friends. Sorry to this man, but I've pinned some rather unrealistic expectations onto him. It's an imaginary relationship that's never once felt real and is therefore completely safe. He's miles away. He's partnered too. It's failsafe. In my mind, I'm imagination-married to Peter. In my mind, it's going great.

Our made-up marriage is problem-free. I don't remember the wedding exactly, but at weekends we often sail on our yacht, and dock in those little towns up the Hudson. I have somehow found white jeans that I like and, more importantly, a cognac coloured suede jacket that fits in the shoulder. In reality people are always telling me to shush, to take it down a notch, but that doesn't happen in my Peter marriage, our days on the boat idle by. Peter is nothing like the guy who keeps messaging me on Instagram to call me a 'yuppie Tory cunt'. Imagination-life is serene, and I don't have the ever-present fear that I'm about to be made bankrupt by single servings of bread and butter pudding from Whole Foods.

In recent years, in real life, outside my mind, Peter's worked out a lot, he's succumbed to the fate of many a gay man and got buff, but our fake marriage isn't belittled by gym sessions and protein shakes. The muscle is there without the work. Imagination Peter loves culture. He loves to paint, or maybe he's good with clay, or maybe he tinkles on the piano on the boat and writes stanzas devoted to me. I am his muse but in a cool way. Sometimes I lay on the piano in a tux and we sing duets. I never miss a note.

Peter inspires my writing too. I'm not pretentious enough to write with a quill but I manage a really nice Parker rollerball with blue ink for flair. Radio 4 murmurs as I catch up on my correspondences, deftly wielding those envelope knives posh people have for letters, a dressing gown revealing an appropriate amount of ankle, the prefect balance of sense and sensibility. I don't know if I work from a cabin office with a porthole or on deck, or where Peter is at this point because fantasies don't have the same rigorous continuity as Hollywood films. But the day unfolds as I effortlessly deposit 1500 words into a Word doc. Often we meet for sundowner drinks on deck, something amber coloured in a tumbler as the stars come out. There's Fourth of July fireworks every night, which, being an American, Peter loves, and we eat charred sausages from the barbecue (meat not being problematic is the ultimate fantasy). Halfway down a rum sour he kisses me.

Do we all dream of the lives we don't have? Not so much covet what we see, but construct a fantasy with a minimal base in reality? We can make ourselves potty dreaming of the one that got away, though I don't think the rimming-to-the-point-of-poetry guy was a missed opportunity. But getting dumped always shuts down a route into the future you were banking on, leaving a huge 'what if' in its path. An imagination marriage is a benign antidote to reality, an impossible dream encased in amber, never stress-tested by the stress of real life. It's a nugget of yearning that you can massage whenever it takes your fancy. There's a safety in the fantasy marriage, less the one that got away, more the one that never-was.

I have a wee confession. I actually met real Peter in the flesh once. I convinced him to take me out for lunch in Manhattan on his work account while I was on a commission in New York. We met at some expensive vegan place and the similarities between us were startling: same height, same bomber, we'd both just given up sugar, we even had the same fucking shoes. Rather than a fear we'd human centipede after the main course (no pudding, because sugar ban), my main takeaway was that real Peter can never meet my real Richard, my real husband. Real Peter and I are so startlingly similar I think real Richard would leave me for him, a massive curveball for my imaginary marriage, a total catastrophe. I can see it all so clearly – Richard and imagination Peter on the boat, gazing at the fireworks and feeding each other chunks of sausage, making out after sours. I actually feel a bit sick. I am able to survey this hideous scene and also be miles away and alone, continuity be damned. Cut to me somewhere much less fancy dining by myself, probably lobster and fries to cheer myself up, and one of those tragic plastic bibs. The lobster may spatter but there's nobody else there to care. That feels desperately sad because it is. Lonely lobster for one. That's the main problem with a fantasy, you can't transfer it to real life, it can't live up to the dream. The more real you make it the less thrilling it is, and you end up alone, crying into your lobster.

The Ghost of Raven Past

Between *Raven Smith's Men* drafts one and two, Angela Merkel has done a splendid job closing the German borders, and limiting entry to non-essential travellers from Plague Island. David Hasselhoff's voice single-handedly tore down the Berlin Wall, but Merkel is stronger. I kept double-checking the website and though some part of me believes in the self-styled urgency of my own need to write, to express myself, I don't think Germany would categorise me as an urgent worker. And I'm not really one for loopholes, travel corridors or back passages. I hate the plausible deniability of loose rules. I want to be good, I want to get through the pandemic with the smug feeling of never having cheated the system, or jumped the queue, or charmed boarder control, so I didn't go back to Germany. I Ubered twenty minutes across London to hunker down, shedding no tiers as I sped across the infected city. Not back to Berlin, sadly, but a Berlin proxy, somewhere as equally arch (or at least it was before you could get a kimchi toastie and an almond cappuccino on every corner): East London.

I arrived three days ago with eighteen bottles of blitzed greenery because, for a reason I'm yet to fully understand, I was embarking on a juice cleanse. The bottles looked fairly inane, but the chlorophyll genie within promised to fuel me, kick me, boost me. I'm a pragmatic person, a realist, I understand the importance of not removing all the fibre from your fruits, but sometimes I just down celery juice unquestioningly, mainly to feel Goop-rich. The part of me that thinks this is hokum has been silenced. I want to believe. 'Cleanse me,' I said to my urns of foliage, 'baptise my innards with this liquid spinach.' Turmeric will aid my rebirth, my ascension. It is now day three and I am both jubilant and suicidal. Suicidal is an overstatement, but I've been on the verge of a scream for seventy-two hours, bubbling up in me from my hollowed-out, juice-only body. I wonder if screaming actually helps the detoxification, if the noise cancels out the hunger? I don't know if you've ever cleansed, but the calorie restriction feels like a slow anxious torture and you can understand why *Big Brother* housemates get so irate about the shopping list tasks. The first day was the worst because I am addicted to caffeine. The withdrawal was criminal. A greyness that wouldn't lift like a sinister fog in a horror movie. I was flatter than the battery in my Tamagotchi, my personality a masterclass in downward mobility. I foetaled on the sofa, sinking like Rose's necklace in the Atlantic. Rather than hit rock bottom, I Googled 'coffee on a juice cleanse' and read the mixed advice. I embraced the grey area and thumbed myself a Leon iced

coffee on Deliveroo. Apparently my dislike of loopholes has a limit, sometimes you *do* have to cheat the system.

Over the course of eighteen juices and as much water as I can stomach, I have fantasised about the primal crunch of hard food to the point of near-masturbation, visualising my dick nestled in the crisp shell of a taco. My imagination ran wild. I don't eat meat but was incredibly taken with the idea of hot and sizzling, slightly caramelising pork sausages, and of running into a café with a firearm and doing a bacon heist, retreating to my hideout and weaving the strips into a meaty lattice. I saw someone plait a salmon like a challah bread on Instagram (I cannot tell you why they did this), and rather than scoff or mock, my eyes brimmed, two streaks of green juice sliding silently down my cheeks. I have taken more than one mucus shit, and not altogether silently, thinking 'this is what it sounds like when doves cry'. The thick cordial of my concentration has diluted as images of dense coconut cake light the corners of my mind, stomping out any flicker of creativity like an overly-aggressive bouncer. I have been watching *Buffy* in ten-minute attention-spanning bursts, and I'm not exactly enjoying it, but I don't have the mental energy to search out another series. I am what the French call *les incompetents*. My husband just texted me 'how do you feel?' and I replied 'great', because what else do you say? 'I feel like I'm dying, shall I go towards the light, my grandma is here and she's telling me to let go'? I'm not expecting great prose until I'm back on solids tomorrow, but here I am writing.

Like a prodigal son, I've returned to East London, my stomping ground for fifteen turbulent years, a fever dream of parties and anxiety. Obviously, I've been back to East London in the five years since I moved South. Nights at the Queen Adelaide with bar muck creeping up my shins, one time dressed as Queen Elizabeth at Balmoral. I've popped East for Sunday lunches, and birthday barbecues. My life migrated South for the late spring of my youth and make no bones about it, I have no regrets. But this is the first time I've been in East London to live, an attempt to prosper. This is the first time I'm not hours away from going home again. I've always been a visitor. A daytripper. A temp.

There's a macabre familiarity to London Fields, made more eerie by my low blood sugar. With lockdown in full force the streets are empty and have the uncanny feeling of a historical re-enactment, a stage set with no actors, the Universal Studios East London theme park. This part of London feels haunted, not so much with my old haunts, but the ghost of me at twenty-five, the spectre of my youth. It's incredibly weird to inhabit the space of the old me, to walk the same streets, and reminisce. This would be the point in the musical of my life where I start singing a poignant melancholy lament but I'm currently too weak to hold a tune.

I was sharpening my pencil for a new draft, but find myself at the beginning of a startlingly recognisable textbook. Like the cold, the ghost of twenty-five has gotten under my skin and into my bones. I feel like I've acciden-

tally put him back on like a familiar coat, but I can't shrug him off. I'm not regressing, I'm just highly aware of the idiot me that once lived here, swaggering around like he owned the place, dressed in incremental degrees as a libertine, as a klaxon, a cobra snake. When people do past life regression they're always Cleopatra or Henry VIII, but I've only regressed a decade and I just see myself, younger and dumber. It's not the series of good or bad memories that's the issue, it revisiting this man-boy on the cusp of something. That sounds like a hammy Ted Talk opener, but I just want to admit on paper that at twenty-five I wasn't the slightest bit bothered what the future was bringing me because I was devouring my locale like Pac-Man. I loved every minute of living in East London. My life had an enchanting pandemonium, the fairytale of being twenty-something, barely a goblin in sight. I was Hansel and Gretel-ing crumbs of experience, and I was too thin for the witch to eat. I'm aware I'm overly-romanticising this period. I'm trying to get some of the joy of my hedonistic twenties down on paper, and I'm struggling because it's not joy I'm feeling now.

Because my life is one jammy episode after the other, I'm hunkered down in a Poirot-esque 1930s German hospital that has been converted into cute apartments. Weirdly, from the roof I can see directly into the bedroom I rented nearly two decades ago. It's a time warp. I am Marty McFly in the future looking back at the past. The room has the same curtains, which someone opens each morning, and

I'm both disappointed and relieved I don't have binoculars. Despite the tiny room, and one flatmate killing himself (we've been into that already), I was quite happy there. Or at least I thought I was happy. And that might be the main, nagging issue with my past self: the ghost of Raven at twenty-five thought he was happy.

When I lived here before I wasn't sad, exactly. You could only really see the unhappiness if you squinted hard enough (or if you're my mum). I wasn't miserable. I was contentedly coasting. I was drifting in very manageable waters, the molten slag of being young, Peter Pan-ing my boyhood, avoiding incipient adulthood. I'm sure I had dreams of a better life, or at least idealised a future, but I never, ever thought beyond the next weekend, the next bar shift, the next party. I was terrified of becoming one of the old stalwarts of the scene. You know the type, they dress young but their eyes have seen decades of revelry, too many dance floors, too many gigs, every year a spring of students descending on the capital. They say everything is shit, that the old days were magical, but they're still out the following night, nursing another pint and that recognisable glimmer of optimism for a good time.

It will surprise no one to hear that my self-care during these years was quieter than a whisper, perceptible only to dogs. I had never done a sheet mask. A splash of water and some face moisturiser that I'd also apply to my legs when it was sunny. My biggest indulgence was cocoa-buttering my elbows in early-August. I got two huge styes in my eyes that

I just partied through and ignored. After a spell (weeks, then months) the swellings sort of solidified into scar tissue. There were eighteen months when I was legally blinded by these lumps, and I kept missing hospital appointments to get them lanced because I slept all day and I was lazy. Eventually, after a stern telling-off from a London doctor, I had to go back to the hospital by my parents' house in Sussex to have my eyelid cashews surgically removed, which turned out cool because the nurse gave me an eyepatch that matched my deep v tee. I don't know how I managed to convince myself I was okay, that I was thriving, my eyelid developing its own cease and desist. Styes were just another by-product of compulsive partying, and I had no intention of letting up. I was literally and figuratively blinkered to myself. I thought I was winning at self-care if I remembered to drink a pint of water before bed. Hangovers were easier managed than cysts.

I couldn't afford anything, either, so my options were limited. I made just enough money to cover my rent. I remember agonising over a shirt that cost £25 from Topman, trying to pre-determine the myriad times and ways I could style it. For all the people who've weaponised their critique of fast fashion, don't worry, I still look for longevity in a garment, it's not a wasted skill, but I don't wake up anxious that the Topman shirt doesn't go with my patent loafers after all. To stretch my dollar, I raided charity shops for the emperor's old clothes. I raided skips. I once did an art project where I got people to pretend to be me and someone said 'everything you own is stolen or found in a bin' which is a fair assessment of my compulsive magpie-ing. I was always looking for a shiny treat.

The past is a fertile place for empty speculation, and I find myself indulging. Being in East London again reminds me of the opportunities that sailed by while I was convincing myself I was flourishing. During these years at my most hot but least happy, I was quite proud of achieving relatively nothing. I made wrong decisions in haste in the small windows I was awake between night shifts. I was sleep deprived because I thought sleep was for fucking idiots. Much like now, it was a time when people thought they were very cool but weren't. Trying to get into *Purple* in clothes manufactured in downtown LA. You might, on certain nights, find yourself in an East End club thinking 'when did everybody start wearing Taliban scarves'? I met good, decent, Taliban-scarf-wearing people and instead of getting to know them, instead of building closeness, I just danced away from them. I abruptly knotted relationships to avoid any overthinking or real feeling. I made baby steps into deep, intense friendships with brilliant women full of laughter and camaraderie, and then sort of dropped them, cauterising the friendship when it got too real, too caring. I couldn't commit to the intensity. Something always held me back.

Sure, I had the naturally supple skin of a twenty-five-year-old (something I'm still chasing with retinol) and an absolutely killer arse, but I had no career. Those fleeting career opportunities, few and far between, were never caught. I had nocturnalised my life, and internalised my potential, living in quite a small feedback loop of partying and sleeping, with obligatory breaks for bar work, spending the deposit for a starter home on Kate Moss for Topshop skinny jeans. I think of how badly I ate and how heavily I drank. And how, by trying to enjoy everything, I ended up missing out. I was in a rut but the rut was glittered and the music was good. I was too busy dancing to notice my own stagnancy, doing the running man on the spot. This is the ghost I'm faced with now I'm back, he is the fathomless opportunity I squandered because I just wanted to look nice and go out. That's all that mattered.

This feeling of remorse might only be a product of my current state of inadequate nutrition. My body is detoxing and I'm inundated with memories where my blood toxicology would make George Best blush. My stomach rumbles and it's easier to regret the past and ignore that it was massively fun. The kind of rootless fun you only have when you're rootless. More fun than I could handle now. I have a piercing guilt over my between-party malaise. All the nearlys are agony. But was it a waste? Was it abnormal? Did I squander my youth or live through it the only way the young can? I'm being quite hard on quite a normal twenty-something, a man-in-waiting who didn't know exactly what he wanted, but knew what he enjoyed, living a life in the shortest of terms and investing nothing for the future. Perhaps I should cut him some slack? I possibly didn't have the maturity to see what was happening, let alone evolve out of it. It's difficult to find any long-term fulfilment, to know what that means to you, when you don't really know yourself. And I didn't have a handle on my heart's bubbling desire, I swallowed it down and chased it with gin. Life was smacking me in the face and I loved it, I really did, but now I'm looking down and I can see the nosebleed.

Find me the twenty-to-twenty-five year-old that isn't a dick and I'll show you a liar. Or maybe not a liar, but someone whose priorities are immature, at odds with their adult body. Someone who's so imbued in their own immediacy that they can't properly future. All reaction, no investment. They make deliberate decisions that are exciting and toxic, that's the whole point. They leap into corrosive situations and scrub the acid onto the most stinging parts of their skins just to see how it all feels. They don't sleep and rest and savour. I'm not completely sure how I made it to today, to be sitting at a desk deliberately challenging free radicals. It was incremental, rather than severe. Everything is such an effort when you're hungover and yet I was able to cap the fear of missing out, to spend my energy building something that lasts. It took something (I'm not sure what) to quit the night job that didn't serve me. To actually start writing. And in turn to truly believe I'm a writer. Maybe the definition of being twenty-five means not quite having your shit together and maybe that's okay. You just take what you're given and roll about like a dog in fox shit.

The Misogynist Who
Came to Tea

I always dream of having huge family dinners like the opening credits of *Roseanne*, where everyone's slingshotting stodge and wheeze-laughing with their mouths full. Something about not being able to hear myself chew over my raucous offspring feels thrilling. Circus-y and messy in a cool way where I have flour up my arms like I've been fisting a pizzeria and my apron's Myra Hindley portrait-ed with different tomatoey handprints as I do a that's-family-life-for-you-shrug. There's ricotta because ricotta is the cheese for the free-spirited. And gingham somewhere. A joyful, manners-free eat fest. Kids with bolognese lip liner. Something accidentally smashes and we all cheer. Everybody stuffed like a vegetarian's red pepper. (I somehow wake up to an operating-theatre-clean kitchen the following morning.)

Currently my home meals are quieter, with a touch too much Maldon salt. It's not too shabby at home because of Netflix and my cat, and sometimes eating with just a fork on a stool in front of the telly, or sometimes a chardonnay in the bath and the short roll into bed. Being at home in your comfies eating bowl food is the closest many of us will get to the relief Victorians knew when a quack doctor prescribed a trip towards the equator and plenty of fresh air after a bout of flu. I'm capable, at an extreme push, of knocking up an incredibly fussy Michelin star-adjacent meal at home on a Saturday night, but I'm not a food snob. I've made that viral TikTok pasta, too, though that's less in line with the palate one might associate with an esteemed former salad-pudding chef.

So yeah, dinner at home is grand but, my God, I do love a dinner out. I love not checking the fridge and not trying to be imaginative. I love not nipping out to buy one last thing for a depressive omelette (eggs are depressing when enforced). I love not being in harsh supermarket lighting. I love being waited on. I love a pre-drink. And a starter. I love a cocktail made of food. Even though the most raucous of restaurants bulk at bolognese lip liner, I love a saucy main, something perilously drippy. I love sides, obligatory greens with my fish, mash with my pasta. I love £8 puddings, I really do. I love dinners that taste so good they become anecdotal mastication, and I love sharing stories of my week, an anecdotal masturbation. I don't love when the bill comes, but I love the silent receipt division between friends or when somebody who only drank cocktails throws their card down for all of us. I love not washing up. I love the consensual slap of a slap-up meal. It's just as nice having bar tapas over a few hundred wines, repeatedly texting your partner you're about to leave, yes, you're in the Uber, you're right outside the house. I also like the buffet at a party

(Halloween, birthday or pool). People are quite rightly buffet-mad, I like to watch them returning for more like pigeons pecking at fried chicken in Dalston. For me, the best dining tends to happen near or over water. I celebrated my thirtieth at a Bond villain's lair in Barbados with manta rays circling the water below, then back to the Airbnb for a goldfinger. Nothing comes close to the top deck feeling you have when you can hear waves as you chomp. Even on a choppy day, it's brilliant dining on a boat (the end of the pier works too, at a push). If you're on a luxury cruise, you should order something marine: fish or scallops or oysters. If you're in a lifeboat waiting for rescue, then it's the strict emergency rations of a dry cracker, half a sip of your own piss and a lick of flare as pudding. You thankfully don't need to worry about salt. There's really nothing gourmet about survival.

Wherever I'm dining, I always eat the warm roll and butter before the meal. It doesn't matter what I've ordered to follow (usually something under a carpet of parmesan), pre-bread is a must, it's clearing your throat before you sing, it's possibly the best part of dining out. I'd gladly add bread to my close friends. Like a girl who sleeps around in high school, bread has an unfairly bad reputation, it became unpopular. It was LA, I think, that first turned on gluten and outlawed boulangeries.

Have you ever had high tea with a misogynist? I have, and we'll get to that. But you have too, we both know it. Maybe not a high tea, rare and expensive as they are – the fingers of cucumber sandwich that cost eight quid, intricate and ornate as Ben Affleck's back tattoo, the bagless Earl Grey, the squared sugar. You probably met your one at a dinner and he (it's always a he) seemed nice at the beginning. He was charming and dashing and, dare I say it, suave? He twinkled lightly on the conversational piano of small talk, he knew the right fork for the salad. A good friend always stabs you in the front, but misogynists tend to creep in under the door as you're settling into a digestif. They look like normal men, but normal men they are not. The never seem like pricks at the get-go. There might be a light comment about woman being *loud* or he'll say *female* CEOs (one actually boiled my piss like a lava hitting the sea when he said to me that female CEOs were shit because every month their hormones surge and they can't make rational business decisions). The misogynist may well venture into the deep waters of trans rights. He might say 'bumboy'. He's not a full Incel, they're quite rare offline luckily. He could be a disciple of the late-stage laddism, a fourth wave lad, who'll claim his insults are merely banter. He'll imply women should be smaller, should take up less space. When they're not pouring themselves into smaller and sexier dresses, women should be making smaller sounds, smaller smells, discreetly bleeding in a locked bathroom. He is a poltergeist lobbing casual sexism across the room, and chipping at the atmosphere with a gentle chauvinism. But he's de-masked, you've foiled him like a Scooby Doo villain. He would have gotten away with it too if it wasn't for that corrosive misogyny seeping from his pores. He always has friends who defend him, that's just what he's like, they'll tell you. You've met another one. Misogynists are like salt, they're hiding everywhere.

Sometimes you're out in Brixton eating pretentious fried chicken because Brixton has had an influx of rich people and they expect their fried chicken pretentious. Established Brixtonites watch you pay fifteen quid for drumsticks and fries. I spent a lot of time in Brixton as a yoot dem. My dad lived there and I'd join him every Sunday for a walk round the market collecting bun to sustain my Brighton life. I remember those single days and occasional weekends more in freeze-frame, but the images are faded and shuffled. We never really *did* anything, we never planned, never plotted. One hazy summer week I went to stay with him, and he was surprised to see I'd brought my swimming trunks because, I assume, it's too difficult to actually do stuff over half-term with your excitable seven-year-old. On the daily walks round Brixton, I didn't realise that the fist bump he was doing with the people we met was meant to be just a touch, so I spent a few days punching their hands as hard as I could. He noticed, I stopped. I don't remember a single other event that week outside of sitting in his flat with the telly on and music on and him reading the paper. Oh, he made me Weetabix with hot milk which I didn't eat because that's disgusting. And then he made them for me again the next morning. And the next. Not cruelly Victorian by any stretch, no need for a quick call to Childline, but incredibly un-attuned to the needs of a little boy (embryonic man). All I wanted was cold milk on my cereal and a swim. Well, I say that, but it doesn't quite cover my deep, deep need for fatherly attention. I appreciate parenting is quite intense, especially if you have an aggressively expressive boy on your hands and you're used to living alone, no woman, no crying in a one-bed council flat. Your entire estate may be shook by this miniature Liberace for a week. But a child's chronic intensity and expectation are diluted by chlorine. Throw him in the pool and take an hour off, Dad. This didn't happen. I was disappointed and bored. The market walks were the highlight.

It is in the market where we lay our scene. I was with one of my most feminist friends, and by that I mean most vocal, and by that I mean normal. It is incredible that in this day and age, with all the wokeness and pop-feminism Instagram accounts and general access to information, that I have friends who aren't outwardly feminist. They don't want to challenge the patriarchy, they want to quietly survive it. Women who live feminist lives on feminist shoulders but would never chat feminism. I do see the appeal of coasting, but it leaves the next generation equally as fucked, not exactly pulling up the ladder behind us, as re-laying the glass ceiling and hiding in the attic, pretending there's nobody downstairs. We don't get a female president by ducking out of a confrontation, by swerving difficult conversations, by letting things slide just this once. Every little helps. Anyway, me and my feminist friend were mid-way through our pretentious chicken when my husband showed up with a noted misogynist. I'm trying to remember how I knew he was a misogynist. It was always uncomfortable when he had a small drink and ogled women, there was that. There was some talk of him fucking his maid? There was his having a maid (his terminology, not mine). Inconclusive gossip, sure. But there was something in the way he split women and men, the way he operated with each was different. I appreciate this isn't inherently evil. He always acted like the lead man in his own movie (I can be guilty of that), but he was Bond and the women were always Bond girls, disposable and replaceable, never invited to stick around after the pussy galore. He did eventually fall in love, get his heart broken, and he softened over time like a biscuit. But at this time he was fully cadding London, the only narrative his dick, his conquests, his next woman. Needless to say, he wouldn't have been my first choice to invite for ostentatious chicken drumsticks with an outward feminist.

Richard didn't mind any of this, or didn't see it, or didn't think it was a problem. He doesn't always necessarily see problems coming over the hill, he tends to notice the iceberg once it's been hit and the hull of the boat's caved in. He couldn't see it was like bringing heroin to a children's tea party: not unfun, per se, but wholly inappropriate. Unlike heroin, the misogynist didn't make us all feel sublimely happy, painless, detached or relieved. He arrived three-pint-horny, that ogle-y stage I knew to not be good. I tried to keep things civil, knowing that oil and water don't mix, except in a vinaigrette. I guess I was hoping for a vinaigrette conversation, but what I got was insoluble fibres, separate and divided. I let out a groan so faint I could have pretended it was my chair, as the slow-motion catastrophe unfurled in front of me.

Now, such is the intoxication of Brixton chicken and rum punch, that I can't put my finger exactly on what went awry. This is frustrating for me too, because I am an avid trader of juicy details and time passed has robbed me of this particular juice. I want to say he said something awful about women and the misogynistic house of cards collapsed, but it was almost my fear of something awful being said that derailed the night. There was no confrontation, no 'female' CEOs can't do their jobs commentary, just a great unease, a few clunky chords of the *Jaws* soundtrack but no sign of the shark. Was anything loaded (like our fries) or was it just me, my background knowledge of him and her? Could I hear his misogyny or her feminism in the lightest of interactions? There was a mutual half-conscious realisation on each side: she the woman who wanted to be spoken to normally, equally; he realising she wasn't a conquest, another notch, she wasn't available to him in a way he could comprehend, she didn't serve his limited requirements of women. I know this sounds toxic, and it is, but it's impossible to tell the smudged line between how I anticipated they might be feeling and what was actually occurring. There was nothing to call out, no shots fired. Just two people with wildly different world views meeting for the first time and finding the common ground lacking. This is not misogyny, is it? Two people not quite clicking happens. Somewhere near you this very second two people are not-clicking, awkwardly unclicked. What they don't need is me interjecting to explain their politics.

In the meantime, I squirmed and squirmed, the chicken congealing on my plate. I could hear a sort of 'do you bite your thumb at me sir' speech between them but it was all internal monologue. I wonder if there was something I could have done or should have said explicitly? It was a thick atmosphere, like a slice of blancmange, that we were all trying to see through (apart from my husband who was classically oblivious to the mounting tension, and foraging for chicken scraps on my plate). I felt like I couldn't say anything, because the elephant in the room was a feeling, not a solid thing with a grey trunk and a circus procession. Had she fully Scooby Doo-ed him? Foiled his plot? Or did he just seem drunk, a bit of a dick? I have, at times, been accused of overthinking. This meal was an overthinking championship.

There was no showdown, because nothing was explicit, but maybe that's the power of misogyny today? It's mutated into a quietness that goes undetected. You hear a few bars of *Jaws* but never the full shark. What a miserable thought. It's not often you get CEO menstrual cycles explicitly criticised, that's why it gets mentioned repeatedly in an essay. And part of me held back over the chicken, part of me didn't want a fuss, part of me wanted to coast as unbumpily through this dinner and out the other side to the safe space of my feminist life and talk of Hillary Clinton and toxic hun culture. I have my own relationship with misogynists. There's a weird code of masculinity, of all men, that I can't *not* be a man within. I can't *other* men, I am one, and when I call out their shitty man stuff I become less of a man, more of the enemy, the opposition. Men are a club I still don't have the full set of keys to, and openly questioning their motives with women reduces my own masculinity, which is fine but also not fine at all. It's not always comfortable to dismantle the poisonous freedoms of my own gender, my own sense of self. Once on the train home from school this boy asked me, 'do you actually like girls' company?'. And all I could think was, 'they don't ask me shit like this'. But it's not that simple. There's an insinuation within the question that I'm less of a man, less masculine, by way of fraternising with, if not the enemy, then the opposition. And I can't think of men simply as pure opposition, of masculinity as something outside of myself. Looking down and seeing my own dick prevents that easy distinction.

Are men the criminal masterminds? Have we reached a stage where we're careful to challenge them because every one of them is a potential ally in dismantling the patriarchy? Are we so keen for comrades that we minimise ourselves, our arguments? I have an internal battle between myself and my masculinity, limited and supreme as it can be. How much of my own masculine power am I willing to surrender in the pursuit of equality? How silent can I remain if it doesn't explicitly interfere with my dinner? Am I pouring myself into a smaller space, just to survive? It doesn't feel right, which explains why a reasonably non-eventful chicken dinner still plays on my mind after eight years. I should have said something. I am guilty of the quiet feminism, the choice to be quiet a privilege in itself, because as a man in that situation it wasn't my gender that was under gentle attack, it wasn't my gender being undermined. I should have challenged the low hum of misogyny. And I could have easily blamed myself for not stepping up, for not acting. But obviously, I didn't do that. I didn't blame myself. I blamed my husband, for that's what husbands are for. To this day we still talk about that night, the awkwardness, the insoluble mix of him and her. I still find it incredible Richard thought his dinner date was a good idea, that as the captain of this Titanic he couldn't see the iceberg. We still haven't decided if this was a bad night or if it was fine. I will say 'well that was awful', and he will say 'no, no it wasn't'. I will say 'I've written about what happened that night in my book', and he will say 'he's not a misogynist, Raven, you're overthinking everything again'. Note to all the husbands out there: never bring a misogynist to dinner, you'll never hear the end of it.

Lean-In

Dig if you will the picture, of you and I engaged in a kiss. One when we first wake up, before I've had a chance to brush my teeth; one when one of us leaves the house for another day of serial emailing; maybe a garlicy one, in the crevice between dinner and sex; our lips locked in matching lifejackets on the bow of the Titanic before it sinks. A kiss is punctuation in the lifelong stage production of love, two soliloquies coming together.

Is there anything more embarrassing than someone *not* returning a kiss? Your tongue in their empty mouth, searching for a response, for vital signs like an episode of *Holby City*. A one-way kiss can feel like a toilet snake down a U-bend. Like a slug in a crawl space. An echoey panic room. One kiss is all it takes, but two people have to be complicit to make it work. These partisan kisses don't happen in the movies, two people are always secretly in love with each other whether they know it or not, the entire narrative onscreen is just foreplay for that first returned kiss. Hold me, thrill me, kiss me, kill me. Maybe I can blame the movies for my kiss failures, because Hollywood warps the reality of love. It's *Lady and the Tramp*'s fault. It's *Pretty Woman*'s. It's Britney and Madonna's (not technically a movie). I blame cinema for making my kiss pre-amble more of a pre-scramble, and perpetuating that ominous idea of 'stealing a kiss', which is cut through with menace. Kisses are things to take, rather than share? Cinema taught me that everyone wants to kiss me but can't quite find the words. If every character is gagging to be kissed, how could I possibly tell if someone real doesn't want to?

I want to somehow make amends to those poor unfortunate souls, casualties of the lean-in. For the sheer awkwardness of me trying to kiss you when you'd rather be in an Uber home, mouth laced with welcoming kebab. For each time I misread the signs. For speeding forward on a red light. Leaning in to kiss someone who's not up for it is absolutely mortifying. Especially if you peek for a split second and see terror in the whites of their eyes. You've gone inside the equations in someone else's head and got the wrong calculation, the wrong answer. Eligible bachelors may have come and go and I would not have noticed, my eye trained on some less eager victim. Victim makes me sound predatory, which isn't the case for these miserable moments, this is much more of a cack-handed tower of Pisa lean-in with absolutely no return on the investment. More pantomime villain than serial creep. I'd like to think these kisses were all glimpses of the sugary sweet follies of youth, but I appreciate the tartness of an unwanted kiss. I've never cajoled or coaxed when a kiss isn't returned, I've just stayed absolutely still like

I'm being hunted by jungle cats, and waited for the ground to swallow me up whole. Please God, may this essay exorcise my lean-in shame so I may walk this earth unburdened.

I have no ingrained inability to woo. I have no skills for it. I was never a notorious Lothario, nor a top shagger. I never had a string of Saturday night dates, or love interests to juggle on a carefully timed rotation, like scheduled teachers to meet on Parents' evening. I was never Peter Stringfellow. And even though I can see that being a Casanova as a long-term scheme is emotionally net negative, I would have liked the choice to opt out of numerous, varied, novelty shags. Annoyingly I came of age in the golden era of pulling, a society set up for emerging adults to copulate. All the clubs, all the foam nights, all the belly tops, all the *Streetmate*. You'd think I'd have learned the ropes while reading *More!* magazine and guides to 'sealing the deal' in *Loaded*. It was a time of great gendering, but that division exacerbated the desire to fuck. Pre-shagging was in the air, an opaque gas, rather than invisibly online. There were lads and ladettes. Everyone was boisterous and up for it (booze and sex). Everything was up for grabs (apart from sleep, you bore). Breakfasts were big. Fatboys were slim. Zoe Ball was pictured swigging Jack Daniels in jeans en route to her wedding. We had metrosexuals, a predecessor to spornosexuals (men who sportily conditioned their bodies into a pornographic aesthetic). People read *Nuts* unironically. Children's TV presenters took their kit off in *Nuts* unironically, because it was a public graduation ceremony from *Blue Peter* and entry fee to post-pub primetime TV gigs. Brands started marketing products that had no Y chromosomes in rigorously gendered campaigns. Yorkie – which I think of as the eunuch of chocolates – was not for girls. We all ate Man Crisps, and drove past billboards of humongous and inviting *Hello, Boys* breasts. Cadbury's had a drumming gorilla that reeked of testosterone. Clubbing was a legitimate personality, like pizza is now. We'd go out to dance (code for cop off). Everyone learned witty-but-quasi-misogynistic chat up lines (unlike today where you're lucky to get a 'u up?' text at 1 am). When you kissed someone, in an inebriated multitask before the dawn of social media, you had to try and remember their face and get their number. Watching your mate get her phone out and share her number with a guy would elicit a cheer. Flirting was a sport. Chirpsing was encouraged. But there were different grades of schmoozing, and some people had all Class As, while I smoked nutmeg through a cloggy bong. Perhaps it was the rampant straightness that inhibited my erotic potential? My potency was somehow diluted in a sea of straights, cut with teething powder, decriminalised. I watched the greatest players of my generation playing, but I couldn't muster the catalytic conversion from fellow clubber to awkward breakfast date. I was forever pre-coital. Courting always feels like a dance I never quite learned the steps to, I never found the beat.

Internalised homophobia was rife in my early dalliances, I think that's what held me back. Objectively being gay was fine, I had come to terms with the idea of it, but I felt like a driver who'd only passed the theory test. I was okay with the sex act itself, the frotting and the transference of bodily fluids, but I wanted the intimacy of two people, the little glances, the micro-affections, the tender pillow talk. It's hard to convey that in any real way at 2 am when the lights come up in a filthy beer-room and there's already a cloak-room queue. I'd love to say the lean-in kiss is a product of drinking, but I stand by the adage (usually applied to bar brawlers) that if it's not in you when you're sober, it won't come out when you're drunk. I was imbued with an incredible neediness that couldn't be contained when I'd had a pint or two. During the day, I was a functioning safe-aholic, anti any expression of vulnerability, suppressing the openness it takes to be seen and loved. In an act of bizarre retaliation to the fathomless possibilities of the gay experience (if only you can let yourself go), I started to think of myself as a superior type of gay, and by that I mean a straight guy who happened to like men but certainly didn't need them. Liking men was a cool strength, but broadcasting my emotional availability like an estate agent was my Achilles heel, the weak link in my personal brand of being fun and carefree. I was terrified of being read as gay from a distance and in turn distanced myself from other gays. I could potentially put a man into my mouth or arse, but not into my heart, because it felt like a threat to my very being. Rather than allow men in, I just got very, very emotionally insular, with explosive pockets of 'please, please kiss me, I'm incredibly lonely'. A detonation of vulnerability that was so intense it cancelled out any potential horniness from a suitor. I remember a guy saying 'I like you but you're so needy', and promptly circling a party asking everyone I knew if they thought I was needy, which might be the neediest outcome. Despite a rigid commitment to coolness – all skinny jeans and fuck tomorrows – I somehow couldn't manage to play it cool with men. I was too locked down, and then suddenly too unlocked, scrabbling to close the gate after the horse bolted. I was never emotionally ajar and intriguing – the base code of any Lothario. Rather than throwing up a warm flume of flat gin and tonic on the pavement, I was Niagara-ing brutal honesty. Honesty is great once you're married because it's the key to a true union, but getting to the altar, or just to the bedroom, needs some mystique. Mystique here means a web of half-truths and gaps in knowledge that the other person fills with projected fantasy. I am annoyingly unpersuasive, the opposite of an *Apprentice* candidate selling a used car. I'm blag-free. My last true blag was years ago, when they'd run out of able-bodied tickets, so I borrowed a wheelchair to see Stephen Fry do a live reading from his autobiography at the Royal Albert Hall. I still lie awake at night thinking of the true wheelchair user at home that evening because the last ticket was sold to me. People talk about where they'd go if they had a time machine – killing Hitler is top of the list – and though I'd love a chance to see the Great Fire of London, I would simply stop myself purchasing that Fry seat. This is definitely going to come up on judgement day. But blag-guilt aside, I'm not one for smoke and mirrors. For falsehoods and fantasies. In a way, I was deliberately not getting good at pulling because it felt so staged, so fraudulent.

I occasionally pulled, but I certainly didn't learn to pull, I didn't glean any understanding of what another person might want. I didn't make the time to learn the trade, to examine the nuances of courtship, because they all felt like micro-assaults to my sense of strength. I was a rock. I was an island. I didn't need joining to the mainland. I have no idea what I was doing while everyone was learning the foxtrot towards the bedroom. I guess I was just at home, covered in burger sauce, harbouring crushes for straight men. Despite my aversion for traditional gayness, I inevitably joined the ranks of the most foolish: the gays who fancy straights. The delicious flavour of unrequited love is that it keeps you completely safe because it never has to survive outside the fertile incubator of your own mind. It's a clever thing, your brain, hitting you with MSG-enhanced emotions without you ever having to be even the slightest bit vulnerable. You feel a lot of feels without ever having to wax. It's not that boring stuff like work seeps into real love, it's that in an imagination relationship you only have passionate arguments (that you always win) and you only have passionate sex (that never hurts). There's a way in which you can construct an entire fantasy around a straight man and the reason it's not happening is because he's straight, so you never have to address any flaws in yourself apart from being the wrong gender. It's a piercing, insurmountable pain, but my God it's addictive. The closed circuit of your desire versus the straight's most basic instinct. The relationship is a theory that can't be road-tested. Everyone has a fable of a straight man turning gay for the right man, but these tales just perpetuate hope for naive adolescents. It's worth saying that a guy with a dick in his mouth isn't *straight* straight. But sexuality is a spectrum and as long as you're happy, I'm happy. When you're suppressing your need to be vulnerable, straight men can seem like the path to salvation, but they're the quickest route to melancholy.

I have always had this underlying feeling that I'm not pretty, not in a conventional way. I've always been a tall glass of water, but I don't think I'm alone in being post-adolescent and secretly thinking I'm ugly. Like I was making do with what I had, rather than flourishing in a way someone would put on the cover of a magazine. I know capitalism is set up to make us feel unpretty, like we're not enough. It keeps us hooked on the promised elevations of under eye rollerballs and jazzy shirts. Traditional archetypes of beauty centre on the blonde and blue-eyed and I was the opposite of that, something I now try to wear as a badge of honour. My un-run-of-the-mill un-boringness. I boast that I'm an acquired taste, but I'd still love a day being catalogue hot and turning straight men into my playthings. I'm unconventionally handsome maybe, and definitely tall, which is a bonus. My early twenties were completely different to my late teens, when I finally started to realise the power of my differences. I could make attractive my own like an *X Factor* cover. I started pepper spraying people with my personality. I water cannoned new acquaintances with wit. I realised I had about ten seconds to pour a glass of sparking personality for a potential mate, before I'd lose them to someone prettier and quieter and less funny who left more gaps in the conversation for romantic projection. I had a tiny window to vomit my pithiest one-liner before they'd be gone like sand through the hourglass. I didn't realise the superpower of individuality when I was young. I muddled through, and it's a relief to look back and realise that even though I was objectively hotter (teenage collagen is a balm) I wasn't happier, I wasn't closer to people. I couldn't approach anyone with confidence, I couldn't talk with irreverent purpose, I couldn't find the common ground. Instead, in my quest to protect myself, I fell into staccato sentences and leaned in for an unwelcome kiss.

Cleaner

While chipping at the dried Colgate ejaculate around my sink, I dream of a kind woman with a big heart that my husband and I lovingly describe as 'basically family'. A woman that doesn't mind damp towels on the floor or a leaning tower of magazines by the loo. A woman who'll hand wash our predominantly earthenware plates. A woman who'll carefully dust around our mantle of pretentious bits and polish them with ecologically sound products. A woman who cleans. Women historically take on the responsibility for the equilibrium of domesticity, alongside the management of how *everybody* feels. A cleaner slash housekeeper slash Esther Perel type would both polish the silver and soothe us, sweeping up longstanding emotional resentment alongside the cat's hairballs. Would she coach us? Encourage vulnerability? Cleanse our chakras? In my dream she's the therapist from *The Sopranos* with a bucket and mop.

After ten years together, with no kids yet (I bought a robotic Dyson because I love the idea of never truly being home alone), I ask myself what we're doing if we're not morphing the borderline abuse of marriage into the ravages of parenthood? I wonder what turns a couple, just two people, into a family? I thought it was our cat for a spell, someone infinitely more demanding than me, someone we jointly keep alive unlike the withered cacti in the spare room. Or maybe it's shared sayings that make a family, the catchphrases of togetherness? Nearly all of ours are borrowed from *Bridesmaids*, but that's okay. Family catchphrases are only really noticeable when you visit your in-laws at Christmas because you find yourself explaining to your partner why your mum is doing a fake German accent as she stuffs the turkey. But mine and my husband's personal brand of family might not be catty or chatty, it might just need an outsider spliced into our domesticity, grafted onto our daily life. Nothing makes you realise how easily familial you are together as another human in the room, an invader to your privacy.

Relationships go through phases. I met Richard as I was thawing from my Intern Age and we chased free drinks parties across London. We stormed the city's parties, being *very* fun, until someone senior from one of our works would appear from nowhere and we'd scarper before they noticed how drunk we were. Life before cohabitation was a breezy pre-nup where we'd meet up already looking great, dance all night, get Brick Lane bagels, shag, and nip home in the morning for a hangover poo. I cooked for Richard a lot, great vats of shepherd's pie with crushed potatoes and peas, one time with a cauliflower cheese top (I really wanted him to love me). I once served him a rather anaemic looking nutmeg mince and hummus plate, which he *still* says is the best thing I've ever cooked for him. I attempted a duck ragu, which refused to fall off the bone until three hours after dinnertime and left a wet patch of orange oil on the dishes. It was a Meat Age that lasted right up until we moved in together. We find ourselves having now settled into the kind of domestic life you see in Ladybird books, all hand-wash-only crockery we've picked up on our travels. I don't know how it happened, but the two party boys now eat meat-free meals in front of our TV like a Gogglebox couple that've given up talking out loud. And I still can't say with confidence which one of us is responsible for rinsing the dishes.

Richard and I have different roles and we've fallen into a natural pattern of the things we each do and don't do. I wouldn't like to out myself as a full nag, but I'm fairly particular, with an overbearing common sense that does even my own nut in. So there are Richard jobs and Raven jobs. Some things are *responsibilities* set in stone, and some are *favours* to the other person, to the relationship, gifts to the gods of shared living. House rules tend to manifest organically. There's often *an event*, something that disrupts the status quo, that changes the game. Richard's catastrophic destruction of a particularly nice colander was *an event*, and put an end to blithely dumping everything into the dishwasher (in fairness the colander still has holes and drains, but the French country kitchen sheen has been compromised). A more extreme example of *an event* is when I asked him to get rid of the dead mouse the cat had gifted us during a blistering summer heatwave (nearly all issues with wildlife are Richard jobs). The mouse body was thrown straight into the outside wheelie bin without the requisite pass-the-parcel layers of newspaper and double, triple bagging. There's fourteen days between bin collections and I can't, in all honesty, tell you on which day I opened the bin to deposit recycling because the ripe, rotten smell of the cadaver gave me amnesia. I had anosmia till the autumn which is terribly sad (imagine Bonfire Night without the olfactory delights of actual bonfires).

Luckily for Richard, while he shoves livestock into the trash I have an undiagnosed neating disorder where I can't stop tidying up. Artfully arranging my desk. Revising the order of the larder. Alphabetising the bathroom liquids. Everything just so. I like things I don't really have to work at, and neatening up is a mindless reflex. I can tidy a room for an hour, I don't even to need to have a podcast on. I can lose myself in the role of Home Art Director and forget my worries. Cleaning hits differently. I have to engage with the task in hand and I hate it. I do not get pleasure from the wire wool, the microfibre cloths, the using your own fingers to get your own debris out of your own plughole. There's an asymmetrical division of labour in our house, and though I genuinely love the invigorating catharsis of online grocery shopping (Ocado is my Fight Club), I pray for housekeeping respite like Cinderella. I open and close the blinds so many times a day that I'm starting to begrudge them, entertaining the intrusive thought of tearing them all down and permanently black-outing the glass like it's the Blitz. I dream of Shakespearian times when there was absolutely no cleaning and you could live in filth, a river of shit trickling past your house. Many got the Black plague, which feels like a small price to pay, all things considered.

I think of all the time I'd save if pointlessly rearranging my house were off the agenda, if Esther Perel were on standby with a cordless Dyson and I could rethink my schedule. I always want to see celebrities on the tube acting like normal people – sweating to death on the Central Line, eating with their hands, sniping at their partners – and there'd be plenty of time to do a fake daily commute and gaze upon the stars. I'd cook more too, the Nigella of my kitchen rather than the head heater-upper. There's the money I'd make in all those vacuuming-free minutes, obviously reaching billionaire status and shutting down the worst parts of the Internet, enforcing a curfew for right-wing tweets. I'd buy the *Daily Mail* and close it immediately, and defund all hate speech. A Nobel prize nom would come my way. That's the power of adequate domestic help.

We had a cleaner before and it didn't go great. Our first flat was three rooms but even then I couldn't detangle myself from the compulsive neating, fingers bleeding as I moved all the cheeses to one specific part of the fridge. The cleaner was eccentric in a way that made us hire her for entertainment value – in her interview she boldly stated that she was an agoraphobic millionaire, by way of 'playing the online markets', and cleaning was the only thing that got her out of the house. Initially I loved to dine out on her bizarre tales (her son was scouted as 'a potential super-model') but her eccentricity eventually gave me anxiety. Though she changed sheets and hyper-bleached the toilet, I always felt like she was taking notes on our lives while she swept, absorbing clues. She wasn't keen to befriend us, so much as infiltrate our lives, our jobs. I'd never had a cleaner before so I didn't realise you have to draw a line in comms like you're in first class on a redeye and can't be arsed to talk. Because both parties were acting out of role, we became somehow entangled with her relationship with her 'super-model' son, who was careering off the rails like any normal teenager. It was Richard whose skin she really got under, phoning him at work, asking for help with her hare-brained fledgling business (I can't remember the specifics, but she had a brown paper bag with a logo she'd Sharpied on).

I realise she sounds quite sweet, but she was cool and bulldozer-y like crime bosses in gangster films. I was more patient with her, desperate as I was to not return to a life of Dettol-ing, but things deteriorated when she started show-ing up on the doorstep on non-cleaning days, fake crying. It ended in a bizarre face-off at our home, the woman call-ing me 'a brat' and Richard 'a king' (a not unreasonable assumption based on the clues she'd collected while sweep-ing), and storming out the house never to be seen again. I sent her a lengthy text, all understanding and noble, trying to simmer the situation to which she replied 'you are a child'. For months afterwards, I looked for her in the local area, sensing she wanted some kind of vengeance. I was paranoid she'd copied the keys. I was certain she was going to jump out from behind a parked car and throw acid in my face. I saw her months and months later, silently dancing in the street wearing massive headphones at 8 am (I kid you not), and she shouted the single most scary thing you could shout at someone after a showdown in their own home: 'I love you'. When we moved house, leaving no forwarding address, I felt like the end of *The Shawshank Redemption*. I was safe. I was free.

So I'd like another chance at a cleaner. A blank slate. Another bite of the at-home hotel service that replaces the miniatures consumed from the fridge (alphabetically, please) and leaves chocs on the pillow. I'm happy to pay the going rate and tip at Christmas, but there's a level of subservience that makes me wince. Outsourcing something I'm more than capable of is tricky, made more icky by her being a woman. Such are the trappings of my middle-class aspirations, I thought the conundrum of a cleaner was a class issue, circling on what you can afford and your own privilege, but it's a gender one too. Perhaps that's why I want to think of the cleaner as part of the family, welcoming her into our *Bridesmaids* catchphrases. Perhaps it's easier to say 'I want to see my face in the floorboards' to a paid relative. A close relationship eases the sordid topic of coin, of paying a woman, of thinking as cleaning as work to outsource to women. Of course we could always get a male cleaner, but that reeks a bit of lust. A horny duo that thirstily lap up maleness, inviting men in and vampiring their man-energy, the kind of guys that have erotic male art on every wall and 'accidentally' let their dicks fall out their shorts at the beach.

But I do still dream of cleanie. Mr Potts would be nice, or Mary Poppins, clicking her fingers to tidy the house and whistling while she works. Not a modern slave, an equal. Someone the right kind of eccentric to duet with in interludes of dusting.

The Revelations of Raven Smith

I get off on 'realising shit', it is my kink in the same way some men like ball torture.

I love the vigorous nit shampoo of a good realisation, the world shifting beneath my feet, the ground a little softer, less stable. You might feel this way too, sometimes, your focus sharpening like Magic Eye. Seeing the arrow pointing forward in the FedEx logo can change one's world view, as can realising the boy you've been psychoanalysing can see dead people and you didn't survive the accident. Revelations have a habit of surging up like water in a storm drain, saturating you with their clarity, and then receding, all but forgotten. While you're soaked to the bone they feel vital, urgent.

For me, it's been a huge week for realising shit, I'm reeling from epiphanies. The ground beneath me has shifted beyond recognition, it's liquefied and turned to Glastonbury mush. Anything can trigger these world view tilts, normally it's a podcast with a charismatic host, but I also thank my therapist for teasing them out as I lay back in bed and syphon off my emotional effluvium. There are so many things we do together, my therapist and I, that are naff, genuinely naff. Embarrassingly naff. It's annoying me that they work, because most of it sets off my bullshit detector. We sometimes do a visualisation of me floating above a situation to get perspective, like Bowie and the snowman. I always think of the London Eye which I'm sure *means* something. My sessions always involve some tiny assault to my ego (a passing comment, the slow response to a WhatsApp) that has sent me spiralling. My therapist and I do imagined visits to my wiser self, a much more laid back version of Raven Smith who doesn't fret so. I have also identified talismans of wiser Raven so I can carry 'him' with me as I continually fuck up. (It's very meta.) I pencil-scribble affirmations on the wall: 'you need introspection to be a writer, that doesn't make you an introvert'. I do all of these naff-ass things without a note of glibness, make of that what you will. Therapy is incredibly interesting to you as you have it, but sort of boring to read about, so let's not dwell. Just know that the sessions have a cumulative effect, and I have been gathering *most* of my shit together, and managing the percolating anxiety that comes with being alive.

Recently, as I've gained a certain notoriety on- and offline, I've been troubled. This modicum of fame has left me reeling. Where I once happily chatted to a group of actual friends doing private in-jokes, my broadcast has got bigger, my sentiments are amplified, and I've begun to hear myself echoed back. This isn't a bad thing, exactly, and it's not a brag. It's just something that's happening. I like a chat and I like a laugh and new people thrill me, but I can feel a dread brewing. Of being too glib, too insincere, too one-dimensional. Of being simplified by the social medium. I think of my platform physically, a great floor high up where each edge has a sheer drop. I'm not famous enough to get cancelled, so I don't tend to worry about that, but I have this ceaseless irk, this whining gripe: I feel like I'm being misunderstood. I have a desperate need to be thought of as smart, sharp, something more than a knotted string of jokes like a butcher's sausage. My hot takes and witty one-liners condense my thinking. I don't dumb down, but I certainly simplify. That's the power of a good joke, it takes the huge and makes it an easily digestible morsel that tickles the palate. I will stop explaining jokes to you immediately.

When I speak to people, most often in my DMs, I can tell they're disappointed that I'm not compulsively cracking jokes or being sassy, and in certain times, scoff at my intention to be at all serious. If you're committed to touching lives outside your circle of family and friends, you inevitably get your fingers burned, for me this means misunderstanding. You know from this book that I'm more than jokes, more than quips, not an infinite jester, and it's this disconnect that riles me. The me that surfs waves of complexity, and the audience that just want a giggle. It was like this in primary school too – I went out of my way to be funny, and was livid when my occasional sincerity was rebuffed or ignored. Any potential power of my voice was diluted because it always came in a comedic wrapper. I had set myself up as funny, and it stopped me being anything else. The persona eclipsed the reality. I've been able to balance this out as an adult, to be deliberately slower, more measured, realising that sometimes it's better to be thoughtful than quick-witted. Not everything needs a savage retort, not everyone wants a searing hot take. Sometimes people just want to be properly heard, rather than ammunition for your next quip. This, my friends, is one of my revelations.

I've had some spats online – people who are woke to the point of utter joylessness, anti-vaxxers with an axe to grind, men who seem solely focused on banging my husband. As a by-product of notoriety, people say nice things to you. This again is no bad thing, but I find the admiration hard to stomach, deflecting compliments with bulletproof precision. Because I'm human, I have a desire to be loved and affirmed, but when it's presented I sense danger, I imagine unfair bias. They're not praising me, not the real me, they're praising the highlights reel after an entire summer of *Big Brother*. I ask my therapist, 'what if I continue to deflect every compliment lobbied at me until they completely dry up?'. We, as yet, have no counter affirmation, my wiser self is shtum. But something about compliments makes me feel even less understood, like if we're laughing together you're missing my deep wells of, well, deepness.

And then something clicked. I was talking to my coach about wanting love and feeling fraudulent when I received it, and I realised that it's women whose compliments don't hit. Not the men. The women. The Glastonbury mud at my feet was suddenly quicksand. I realised that this whole adoration/affirmation issue was gendered. Women could praise me till the cows came home and I couldn't absorb it because I was still searching for male validation. How fucked up is that? I didn't need to visualise myself on the London Eye to see the fucked-up-ness. I am surrounded by brilliant women, who both support me and build me up. My mother who raised me. Bosses who saw my potential, hired me and promoted me. A circle of friends who genuinely, unquestioningly want to see me succeed. Women are my scaffolding, raising me up, my cheerleaders, urging me forward. Yes, men are cheerleaders too, but it's women who have truly pioneered me. Women are my lifejacket on the rapids of life, and yet I'm still out here searching for male confirmation. The realisation hit with a dull thud (and an unscheduled panic attack).

My own patriarchal conditioning is much deeper than I expected, and actually stating this all out loud feels deeply embarrassing. I thought I had this equality thing nailed. Nail gunned and gorilla glued and sellotaped and paper-clipped. Houdini locked down. I've spent so long deliberately equalising men and women in my mind, getting the bubble right in the middle of the spirit level, actively challenging inequality: the insidious and the overt, the innocuous and the extreme. I've spent so many years carefully living a woke life, so many nights dressing for myself, so many instances proving I'm more than my testosterone, I simply hadn't noticed this critical gender divide in my thinking. You already know this but the genders are equal but different, like my left AirPod and my right AirPod. I don't need to re-learn the brilliance of women, I already know it in my bones, I live it in theory and in practice. But it's men I want to please.

I am a voracious taster of men, with quite the evolved palate, but I didn't realise how much I needed them, how integral they've become to my way of being, to the fluctuation of my emotions. They are my OxyContin. The square footage of real estate occupied by men in my mind would astound you (and they're living rent free, the cads). I'm hoping the men I meet find me attractive. I want the gay men to want to fuck me and the straight men to think of me as the kind of guy they'd fuck if they were gay. I have become a Content Destroyer, with an output of content that sometimes feels hellbent on attracting male attention.

Men come in many forms, and I sniff out more. I find myself squinting at the little avatar on a private profile, wondering if the man has mileage. Screengrabbing the private profile so I can zoom in. Never, ever following the private profile. I appraise dickpics, the length of a shaft measured in coke cans. I see the feral puddles of muscle you meet on apps: young men who've been jaded by scrolling and are doggedly fortified against mainstream mating rituals, opaquely sexual and anti-emotive. The loose men you meet on apps are the worst, and none of them can fuck you worth a damn. They're either twenty-five and terrible in bed, parroting porn, or aggressively assertive, asking to be called daddy in the first message. It's not that I'm not aroused, that I'm above the sexual trigger of absolute filth, but it's the dragon of platonic union I chase too. I think about travelling the world in eighty days as Michael Palin's plucky sidekick. Of being the great man behind every great Obama. I think about Elton on a Berocca day. I assess co-passengers on planes (to the woman on the BA flight whose eyes said 'stop staring at my husband', I'm not the one who married a ginger dilf). I want, in some small way, for these men to fall for me. To want me for my body, or my wit, or my intellect. To think I dress nicely, or hold myself well, or just appreciate that I'm tall. They needn't offer Charles Manson devotion, following me out into the night and aboard a killing spree. I'll take their fleeting respect. I'll take their momentary esteem.

I am not meant to admit this. I am meant to be better. It's an excruciating revelation, worse than the time I wet myself onstage in the school play. A bad bruise on my psyche, a personal stain. I cannot tell you where my need for constant affirmation from men came from, but it may well be the screaming subtext of everything I've ever posted, and possibly – depressingly – everything I've ever said out loud. Getting men to notice me has exhausted my adrenal glands as I vie for their approval, a personal dancing plague with the subtext of 'watch me twirl, daddy'. (I have a slow, icky feeling that this is all stemming from my relationship with my dad, and that all the men I encounter are but mere avatars for that unresolved situation, but I don't have another therapy session until next Tuesday, so I type on.) Men have become a near-constant focus of my attention. It is ridiculous.

In an act of sabotage, I find myself competing with men, comparing myself to them. On days when I do yoga and swerve carbs, I might be feeling quite hot, quite handsome, but scrolling past a picture of Jon Kortajarena can see me derailed like there's a leaf on the line. I'm back thinking about men, how I can be a better one, how I can win more over. Is there a word for this? It is textbook narcissism? (A little voice is whispering 'daddy' again.) Part of me is worried this is a surface fixation, all about sex appeal and appearances but don't fret, some of my biggest male rivals are intellectually annoying too. As someone who's incredibly fond of serenading a group with the sweet ditty of an anecdote, I'm aware that that can become competitive with certain chaps. I have been known to quietly describe a really good mate as having 'too many anecdotes'. Wow, I'm a dickhead. I'm a really bad friend. Tellingly, I never worry that another man could dress better than me, it's never once crossed my mind.

I cannot tell you which of my beliefs are indigenous to growing up under the male gaze, the flora and fauna of the patriarchy. I do not know the moment when this masculinity obsession was conceived. Men are scented candles, I tell myself, and honestly, at this point in our evolution, is anyone actually in need of a scented candle? They're lovely and can enhance a mood, but you can do that on your own, candles and men are not at all necessary. I have to admit that the people I admire most are men. I'm rethinking if that is true because I would happily walk across broken glass for Donna Tartt, I would make a pact with the sea witch for a day warm on the sand with Billie Piper, I'd give it all up for a long lunch with Samantha Jones, or even Annabelle Bronstein. Perhaps it's just that men monopolise. Men monopolise culture and men monopolise entertainment and men monopolise business. Men monopolise success itself. I can hear myself deriding romcoms and romance, deriding pink (but still wearing it), deriding the saccharine sweetness of cute dresses, deriding the female experience. It's not that I don't love those things, that I don't think they deserve an equal footing, but this is society that praises the male forms of strength and resilience, stacking them above all else. I need to watch out for that inadvertent lean into the dominance of men.

Though I can see the fallible truth of men, I can still feel the discrepancy in my approach. I can pen columns that poo-poo masculinity, revealing its myriad and laughable flaws. I can even write books. I can critique masculinity, I can see its moving parts, I can muddle through the privileged maze, but every so often I catch myself. I'm like a babysitter in a horror film realising that the phone call is coming from inside the house. I am the man obsessed with men. What a revelation.

Everything I Know About Men

That's it, that's the book.

It's an odd feeling, flicking back and seeing letters on a page making up a potted history of Raven Smith. On the one hand it feels significant, it feels vital, it feels like the words Facebook staffers use to describe their own newsfeed. I have Rumpelstiltskinned the straw of my life into gold. On the other hand, it feels indulgent and airless, suffocating like the depths of outer space. I am that guy at a party who can't stop talking about himself. While recollecting memories, I've tried to slice through my epidermis and down to the bone, to the bedrock of my relationships with men. For so long, it's been me and my editor picking at these scabs, a thousand tiny cuts, but here you all come to finger my wounds. You'll join me when I cum in my pants at the beach, when I fake being in a wheelchair, when I'm cast in an opera as a singing porno mag. You'll see me and my husband, my virgin larynx, my writer's cock. I don't think I'll ever be properly ready for all of you in here, mudlarking my life, sifting through the silt.

I have been wildly testiculating for as long as I can remember, wading knee-deep in testosterone. You'll read of my eligible oblong years, each liaison lassoed together by a string of pre-cum. The men that gave me butterflies, the men that gave me the ick. There's nothing like an exhumation of old lovers to leave a slightly metallic taste in my mouth, or the gripey tooth fur you get after you've thrown up. I'm wondering what I've really learnt from those experiences beyond not immediately cumming when someone touches my penis? I'm married now, so this tale finally has its principal breeding pair. My book agent has suggested this might be a love story, a navigation of intermittent McDonalds and the frequent, miserable scrolls of Grindr before I found my husband. Are these episodes mere pre-Richard trials and tribulations? I can tell you right now that marriage, with all its thoughtlessly loud closing of the front door every goddamn morning, and always, without fail, leaving the hallway light on like we live in the hall, doesn't feel *quite* like a fairy-tale ending. I can also tell you that the sound of Richard breathing is the soundtrack of my life.

This is, of course, the final chapter, the part where I tell you what I've learned in a lifetime of sampling men, of swilling and spittooning them like fine wine. What have I gleaned from the non-lovers, the fathers and father figures, the teachers and bosses? I would have loved a twist at the end of all this, some Poirot revelation. To have realised I'm lesbian or that this was all a dream or that I'm a ghost. But the only thing I'm haunted by are the men of my past: they are always with me. I wish I had some searing and salient point about masculinity, or a take so hot you'll burn your fingers, or a witticism so potent it impregnates your very being, altering your DNA and exploding from your chest at supper. But I'm struggling to give you a neatly parcelled takeaway, a polystyrene box full of digestible nuggets. Each man has been so varied, so different, it's almost laughable to have lumped them together based solely on their gender. It feels old fashioned.

I'm not sure, having finished this book, if I'm meant to feel cathartic and joyous? Lighter and freer? Or should I feel resentful, or somehow released, de-shackled from the past? I guess, if I've learned anything, it's that I have no quota for men, no full capacity. I can never quite get enough, I never run out of space like a floppy disc. My cup runneth slightly under, I am always still intrigued.

When it comes down to it, I feel relieved. Relieved that this book is finished. Relieved that I don't have to keep atoning for my obsession with men. Relieved that I'm emerging from a pandemic with a manuscript that mentions the global plague only twice, one time in the context of me absolutely loving arse. And absolutely loving arse is its own brilliant thing. In these pages, you'll have watched me blossom from an unsure sapling into the most wonderful faggot. And looking at these chapters I can feel the absolute joy in my homosexuality, I am revelling in it in every sentence. I don't feel a dot of the shame I initially felt when I realised I was a gay man. I can appreciate the privilege of fully shedding my velvet rage, of stamping out as much internalised homophobia as I can. It means something to fully exist and fully express without apology or fear.

So that's it, that's the book. I'm already sorry it's over.